D0903646

SOLDIER OF FORTUNE

The story of a nineteenth century adventurer

Soldier of Fortune

The story of a nineteenth century adventurer

BY ELLA PIPPING

TRANSLATED FROM THE SWEDISH
BY NAOMI WALFORD

Macmillan of Canada
Toronto

FIRST PRINTING

© in the English translation Macdonald and Company (Publishers
Ltd., 1971; in the Swedish text Ella Pipping, 1967

Library of Congress Catalog Card Number: 70-107405

International Standard Book Number 0-87645-050-8

Printed in the United States of America

Published in Great Britain by Macdonald and Company (Publishers)
Ltd., London
First published in Canada by
The Macmillan Company of Canada Ltd.
70 Bond Street
Toronto 2

TO H.E.P.

'*On a review of the sparkling incidents of his brief and romantic career, I still think on him as the creature of a high wrought fancy rather than of sober reality – like a meteor of uncommon brilliancy, which has suddenly illumined the path of my dull existence, and as suddenly disappeared for ever.*'

Contents

List of illustrations

between pages 144 and 145

'Nichts ist zarter als die Vergangenheit, rühr es
an wie ein glühend Eisen.'

GOETHE

Author's Preface

I REMEMBER the very day when I learned my first fact about my great-grandfather.

My beautiful young mother was seated at her high mirror, dressing for a dinner party; we children were admiring the wonderful things of her treasury – a tiny balalaika in silver filigree, a bumblebee of gold and amber. The 'grown-up-things' were of less importance, but we loved to repeat: This you were given when you were engaged to be married! This heavy bracelet, too, you got from our dear papa, but this was grand-mother's, wasn't it? ... Yes, darling ... and she had it from her dear papa ... Oh, no – he did not give her anything like that! ... Mother's voice was strange. Perhaps he was poor, I suggested gaily ... Oh, no ... Oh, yes, he was poor. Again that embarrassed voice. And then ... Now to bed children or you will get cold.

My question had been wrong. But why? I could not understand. Other children, like me, innocently asked awkward questions which their elders never seemed to hear, but, instead, began to talk about my charming, my poor brave great-grandmother.

I began to understand their reticence when a cousin of my mother, the internationally famous suffragette Annie Furuhjelm, wrote her memoirs. But even she was rather vague about the mysterious fate of her grandfather. She only knew that he had been an adventurous and faithless gentleman, very likely with unpaid gambling debts, who deserted his young wife, disappeared to America, took part in 'the Fenian [sic] rebellion' and was executed. He had brought sorrow and shame to his family.

Annie Furuhjelm entrusted all the papers, letters and diaries she had from her mother to the von Schoultz family archives, but first she put a big envelope in my hands and said: 'You may read this before it disappears.' Her mother had received the envelope sealed and had passed it on, sealed. Aunt Annie had scarcely read more than a part of the thick dossier. She could there have learned, plainly stated, the tragic last act of her grandfather's short life. There lay copies of minutes of the trial, the judicial decision of the court. There was a description of the execution, the burial and the last will. There lay copies of newspaper articles and letters. There were the facts of what happened in Canada.

Yet it raised a new storm of questions clamouring to be answered. A lieutenant's commission for Nils Gustaf von Schoultz and his resignation from Svea Artilleriregemente, sanctioned with Royal Grace, were all that the family archives could say about the prodigal son.

After reading the dossier and dealing with the English letters and journals of the family, I found myself looking for two names only – Ann Campbell and Nils Gustaf von Schoultz. Little by little some short quotation seemed to make another, still shorter perhaps, comprehensible. A word expunged, pages cut out, told me even more than enthusiastic or sober statements. But how, why and when the adventure began still remained a riddle.

I pestered Sveriges Krigsarkiv, Svea Hovrätt, Svea Artilleriregemente with questions and always got friendly, comprehensive answers but seldom anything revealing or new to me.

Some weeks at Harvard in the fall of 1948, with a ticket to the stacks in the wonderful Widener Library, made it possible for me – without disturbing busy librarians – to find my way to historical works, papers, obscure booklets and pamphlets, hunting for what I was hoping to find: a possible mention of von Schoultz in connection with the Upper Canadian Rebellion of 1838. To my astonishment I found the name in almost every account of the affair of Windmill Point. Mostly mentioned negatively, but sometimes with approval. My husband led me through labyrinthine catalogues to official documents and newspapers; in Washington, D.C., in the Library of Congress many of my suppositions were confirmed. I went home with a lot of material for the family archives. This, and nothing else, had been the purpose of my copies and photostats.

Many years later, when we spent some unforgettable days with Kenneth B. and Eleanor Murdock at the newly started American Institute for renaissance studies in Berenson's villa, I Tatti, outside Florence, I continued my romantic hunt. It became a delightful Sentimental Journey around places where Ann had lived and where she had wandered with her charming foreigner. Books in the exquisite library of I Tatti finally gave answers to questions which could not be found in Finland. Amiable ladies of the British Council showed us old maps of Florence and its environs. The genial reverend of the English church sent for the volumes where marriages in the congregation were recorded and we were shown a page where, on 20 March, 1834, Miss Ann Campbell was married to Mr Nils Gustaf von Schoultz in the presence of the noble ministers of Britain and Sweden. Finally, Kenneth's car with jolly Gino at the wheel drove us out to Ann's dear Paradiso on Monte Falcone and up to the magnificent former Passi villa, La Loggia, where in Madame Catalani's parlour the two young creatures first met.

When, after years of research, I put down my miscellaneous material – which many expert and kind people had helped to collect and which now consisted of all there was to know about my wayward ancestor's escapades – it had grown far beyond the limits of a *curriculum vitae* suitable to be added to the family papers.

Many pieces are still missing – the very necessary ones, which perhaps could explain why it all went so wrong. Yet the kaleidoscopic fragments show a distinct, fascinating star – a strange human destiny fulfilled. I made it a story for my children and grandchildren. But I can't tell whether it turned out an adventure story, a real one, or a story of young love or a tragedy. Yet it may stand, as a bit of human comedy, strangely timeless and pathetic as all our earthly acting is.

ELLA PIPPING

Translator's Historical Note

UNTIL 1808, Finland formed part of the Swedish realm. It was governed from Stockholm, and Swedish was the official language. During the seventeenth century many of the enfeoffments distributed among the aristocracy by Queen Christina were called in again to meet national expenditure. The few nobles living in Finland, their feudal power thus curtailed, became primarily provincial administrators and public servants.

Largely because of its geographical position, Finland has always been a buffer state, and during the reign of Charles XII (1697–1718) it was ravaged and finally occupied by Russia.

By the treaty of Nystad in 1721 the larger part of Finland was restored to Sweden, but the provinces of Ingermanland, Ladoga and Karelia remained in Russian hands.

In 1808 the Russians invaded Finland without declaring war. The Finnish people put up a courageous but vain resistance against a vastly superior enemy, and the Swedish central government, unable or unwilling to support and reinforce them, made peace with the Russians by ceding Finland to them.

Czar Alexander, impressed by the valour of the defeated inhabitants, made their country a Grand Duchy and promised them a large measure of autonomy based on the Swedish constitution.

Swedish remained the official language, and not until 1918 when Finland became an independent republic did the Finnish language come into its own. The Swedish forms of place-names in Finland are now used largely by Swedes or Swedish-speaking

Finns (about eight per cent of the population), and in this translation the Finnish forms are used throughout, followed where helpful by the Swedish name in parenthesis. The map on page 192 shows some of the Swedish and Finnish place names side by side.

NAOMI WALFORD

I

The Prisoners in Fort Henry

IN the depths of a December night a young man sat down to write a letter:

Kingston Jail

7 December 1838

My dear friend,

When you get this letter I am no more. I have been informed that my execution will take place tomorrow. May God forgive them who brought me to this untimely death. I have made up my mind, and I forgive them. Today I have been promised a lawyer, to draw up my will. I have appointed you executor of said will. I wrote to you in my former letter about my body. If the British government permit it, I wish it may be delivered to you to be buried on your farm. I have no time to write long to you, because I have great need of communicating with my Creator, and preparing for his presence. The time has been very short that has been allowed. My last wish to the Americans is that they may not think of avenging my death. Let no further blood be shed; and believe me, from what I have seen, that all the stories that were told about the sufferings of the Canadian people were untrue. Give my love to your sister, and tell her I think on her as on my mother.' Was this a considerate way of removing a misunderstanding that troubled his conscience? 'God reward her for all her kindness. I further beg you to take care of W. Johnston, so that he may find an honourable bread. Farewell, my dear friend! God bless and protect you.

(signed) S. von Schoultz

To Warren Green Esq., Salina, State of New York, United States.

The young man wrote a few more letters, including one of thanks to the officers of the 83rd regiment for the sympathy and kindness they had shown him during the last grim weeks. His final note was addressed to the wife of his gaoler, no doubt with a view to its being quoted and commented upon:

Dear Madam,

I was told that the three principal things for freedom, elective franchise, Congress and trial by jury, were not given to the Canadians; that they most ardently desired them, and that the whole was ready to rise, but they wanted arms. Everywhere in the United States societies were formed to procure the Canadian brethren these arms; it was also told me that the regular army was ready to join the patriots. The societies in the United States counted upwards of one hundred and fifty thousand members. I went from Oswego with the intention of arriving at Ogdensburg and there get information from General Birge, who they told me was the Commander of the Eastern Division. I was never permitted to land at Ogdensburg, but carried against my will to Mill Point, to which the said General (a mighty great coward) never came.

Now many thanks to you for your kindness, and also thanks to your husband. God Almighty bless you and yours, is the prayer of

S. von Schoultz

Written the night before my execution, the 7 of December,1838.

The dawn that was breaking was overcast, and a bitter east wind was blowing. A gallows had been erected on the glacis on the north side of Fort Henry. The report said:

Last Saturday morning (8 December) the pirate leader Von Schoultz was executed on a temporary drop prepared on the glacis, north side of Fort Henry. He was removed from the gaol in a cart on Saturday morning, accompanied by the two Catholic clergymen who had sat up with him the two nights previous to his execution. He maintained his intrepid demeanour to the last. . . . After hanging an hour the body was taken down, brought back to the gaol and interred in the Catholic burying ground.

Both friend and foe were agreed that the prisoner had deserved a better end. Captain Luard, the British Commandant at Fort Wellington, who had been present at both the inquiry and the execution, pitied this brave man: 'The misguided Pole simply made the mistake of meddling in foreign politics,' he said, and he pitied 'the gallant gentleman, who was as brave as he was good-looking'. 'He might have won great renown had he fought in a more honourable cause.'

Who then was this man – this foreigner, rabble-rouser, fili-buster, rebel, patriot and hero in the cause of freedom? Was he really Polish? Was he a Catholic?

The human label under which one appears before the Almighty may have little importance; and if the Catholic fathers who hurried to his side believed him to be a Pole and thus a prodigal son of the True Church, we might discern therein the mercy of an omniscient God. For the prisoner in Fort Henry, whether Catholic or Protestant, had more need than many another to be allowed to *talk*. His solitude had been appalling, and these men who were bound by the seal of the confessional were known for their ability to listen with gentleness and counsel with wisdom. What the captive may have said to them remains their secret; with them his story passed into the great silence, and the fragments that I have tried to fit together into a likeness of this enigmatic convict are fragments only; they were scat-tered, and have been hard to find.

Mostly they are reflections: images of people among whom he lived, and of events in which one knows – or assumes – he took part. The genuine fragments are either garish or strangely dim; few of them shine clearly, and not one has the translucency of happiness. The man himself moves silently as a wraith among the fellow-players on that stage – until suddenly, on some rare occasion, he steps so tangibly out of the past that the century and more that separates him from us is forgotten.

The prisoner had little time to tell his story. Nor had his

life been long, though from the beginning it had been filled
with drama and adventure. His contemporaries had some suspicion of this, but never certainty. He himself told no one that
on landing on American soil two years before his death, on 18
August 1836, he registered himself as *Nils Gustaf von Schoultz,
Army Officer, aged 28. Swedish Subject.*

2

Born on the Threshold of War

WE must go even further back in time to a little town in the middle of an unknown country: Kuopio, in Finland.

By the end of the eighteenth century Kuopio had acquired a certain prestige: it was the seat of local government and its social life was gay, and determinedly free from stodgy provincialism. The gentlemen of Kuopio never felt far from the university at Turku (Åbo), or from Stockholm itself, the capital of the Swedish realm. They read newspapers that were no more than a week old, and kept abreast of the fashionable literature of the day. They liked music, and formed their own Musical Society on the best model.

When the newly appointed Circuit Judge of Rautalampi took up residence in Kuopio he appreciated his good fortune. He was Nils Fredrik von Schoultz, the son of a poor army officer, Major Fredrik Gustaf von Schoultz, of the island fortress of Suomenlinna Sveaborg, built around 1750 in the Gulf of Finland. As a boy he had been tutored in the house of the widowed Baroness Ulfsparre, with her two sons; and then, instead of entering upon the military career traditional in his family, he had been allowed to accompany his gifted young tutor, Tulindberg, to Turku (Åbo), university.

He read something of everything, but was said to work hardest at mathematics, physics and chemistry. He wrote verse and felt himself akin to 'the wretched genius Lidner', the poet, who was related to his family. He made music and listened to it, and thought only with repugnance about money-making and the future. At last he crammed himself with the required amount of jurisprudence for a career in the Court of Appeal, lured into this by an influential kinsman. But hardly had he settled comfortably into a good post at Vaasa (Wasa) Circuit Court when his father summoned him to Sveaborg, where various military-clerical jobs, 'in exceedingly ill-educated company', were to bring him more money and better prospects. Nils Fredrik bowed to his father's will, and never regretted it. Being a highly intelligent young man, he was entrusted with an increasing variety of tasks, did well, and in due course was appointed County Court Judge.

In that same year, 1799, he was elected to membership of The Royal Swedish Musical Academy of Stockholm. In July 1800 he was appointed chief magistrate at Rautalampi, and later became a member of the Finnish Association of Rural Economy.

In short, Miss Jeanne Henriette Gripenberg made a good match when on Christmas Eve 1800 she married Nils Fredrik von Schoultz. She may even have fancied that she was making her début into the great world when she left her dear Voipaala, her childhood home, and accompanied her bridegroom to the provincial capital of Kuopio.

There followed a few happy but all too fleeting years. Their second son, Nils Gustaf, was not yet six months old when the ground-swell of the great wars on the continent reached Finland. He was born on 7 October 1807.

On 1 March 1808 the Russians broke in across the Finnish frontier in the east, and from that day Jeanne von Schoultz had only brief glimpses of her husband until, as homeless fugitives, they were re-united in Stockholm. First, at the instance of the provincial governor, Nils Fredrik was sent to the defensive positions in the east. Later he drove westward, across unstable and treacherous spring ice, to General Sandels' headquarters, carrying with him the archives of the province and the public funds. Jeanne and the two young children stayed behind; and so it was that little Nils Gustaf, kicking in his cradle, became a near-participant in the dramatic events of the enemy's assault on Kuopio.

In the midst of tragedy came – as so often – a touch of comedy. Carl von Schoultz's memoirs record that on looking through the shattered windows of the Judge's Residence, young Frau von Schoultz beheld a yelling mob of Finnish soldiers and peasants pursuing a uniformed Russian official. She leaned out, grabbed the fugitive, hauled him inside and hid him in classic style among the silken gowns in her wardrobe. She then walked out on to the doorstep to meet and halt the frenzied rabble, who roared at her to hand over the Russian to be put to death.

The young lady, refusing to be intimidated, scolded them for the disgrace they would bring upon the Finnish name in dealing thus with an unarmed enemy; and she at last succeeded in convincing them that they would do better to defend the town rather than cower from enemy bullets in her courtyard.

The defence of Kuopio was feeble and mismanaged, and the town was taken. But the enemy were soon driven out again by General Sandels' men, who maintained their positions both on the frontier and in Kuopio until June. But when Barclay de Tolly attacked with fresh and superior forces, the defenders were beaten back. Most of Kuopio's inhabitants fled with them. Judge von Schoultz was there by now, and was able to get his wife and children away, but all his possessions had to be left behind. Later, Jeanne continued her westward flight with the babies, and made her way to Voipaala, the home of her childhood in Sääksmäki parish. Her husband was sent back to Kuopio, to negotiate with the Russian general.

Von Schoultz was led blindfold into the enemy-held territory, and when his eyes were uncovered he found himself in his own hall. General Barclay de Tolly had set up his headquarters in the Schoultz's empty house. When von Schoultz, his mission completed, took his leave, the general warmly urged him to return with his family, promising him 'complete safety as to life, service, and property'. 'But only on condition that I should swear the oath of fealty to the Czar of Russia without awaiting the conclusion of a peace-treaty. I regarded this as being contrary to my sworn allegiance to my lawful King and to my Country,' he wrote later in his memoirs. Thus he had no choice but to decline the offer. It is known that his house was later looted and burned.

No sooner had von Schoultz rejoined the retreating army than he was sent by Sandels to Klingspor in Uusikaarlepyy (Nykarleby), on the west coast of Finland. Immediately after his arrival at headquarters he was 'against my will and request, appointed and commanded to take over the administration of Vaasa province, as Vice-Governor'. On reading the very first phrases of his description of the place, one cannot wonder at his dismay: 'A town of Residency, recently sacked; a war-ravaged Province, divided and embittered minds, disorganization of all branches of the administration, and the hourly necessities of the Army operating there, made still more difficult a task harassing in itself...'

In East Bothnia the Finnish army continued to retreat. A pitiful attempt was made to relieve the besieged city of Vaasa from the sea. Negligible though this assistance was, it gave the Russians a pretext for 'savage sacking, massacring, ill-treatment and slaughter of the defenceless inhabitants of the town and neighbouring villages'. The vice-governor's next desperate task was to clear the way north and across the West Bothnian border for the fleeing, shattered army. Nils Fredrik von Schoultz never returned to Finland.

Meanwhile Jeanne and her babies had arrived safe and sound at Voipaala, where she was welcomed by her mother and sisters. Her father, Hans Henrik Gripenberg, later Major-General, had been in the field with his two sons since the first days of the war, though in what areas was not easy to tell. The fortunes of war had continually fluctuated; rumours of any victorious action spread quickly and were readily believed throughout the countryside.

Suddenly one day a message reached Voipaala that the General was on his way and expected a good dinner. Which general? Sandels? Adlercreutz himself? Perhaps one or two of the Gripenberg men would be in his suite. Any animal that remained to be slaughtered was slaughtered, and there was much baking, boiling and roasting. Silver and linen that had been hidden away was brought out, and the ladies of the house arrayed themselves in full toilette, as in the days of peace.

Imagine their horror to see that the general who walked up the steps with his noisy staff was none of those expected. It was Prince Bagration, the Russian conqueror.

Dinner was served, however, with the general in the place of honour beside Jeanne. Tradition has it that she was a somewhat silent companion, and it was the general who kept the conversation going. He spoke of the annoyance caused him by the new and energetic governor of Vaasa province, whose orders were obeyed everywhere. Besides this, the man had 'spread a report about the plundering of Vaasa which had exceedingly displeased His Imperial Majesty', exclaimed the Prince indignantly. 'I have set a high price on his head, and I mean to have him, alive or dead!'

Then, it seems, the silent lady beside him smiled, and looked him straight in the eye.

'I hope you will never succeed. I pray to God that that price will never be paid. My husband has done his duty, no more and no less.'

The Prince, it was later reported, was at first taken aback and slightly embarrassed, but charmed. He apologized at once, most amiably. 'Then, madam, permit me to add that should your husband chance to fall into my hands, I shall not forget the hospitality I have enjoyed today, in the house of his lady.'

But swift repartee and good dinners were of little avail. When news of the Finnish army's retreat to Tornio (Tonneå) reached Sääksmäki and Jeanne learned that her husband was now stationed in Oulu (Uleåborg), she determined to follow him before the onset of winter. Once more she took to flight, journeying with the young children through a war-torn, plundered country. Fredrik, her eldest son, may have retained some memories of that experience; he was just seven. But what deep, unconscious impressions Nils Gustaf may have borne through life of this, his first journey into it, we cannot know. It was no triumphal progress.

Exhausted and wretched, Jeanne reached Vaasa on her way to Tornio and Stockholm, arriving there after its surrender and its occupation by Russian troops. She asked the innkeeper to find her a doctor, and the little man who was shortly announced had hardly set eyes on her when he threw himself on his knees and covered her hands with kisses. For this Russian doctor was the man whose life she had saved. He couldn't do enough for her, and himself ran to the apothecary's for medicines. In the end he induced the high command to provide her with a safe-conduct through Russian-occupied territory. After that they never met again. The rest of her journey may have been less exciting, but it was certainly as arduous. All three of them arrived safely in Stockholm.

Nothing is known of their first months in Sweden, but some of Jeanne's great-great-grandchildren have experienced similar interludes in their lives and can imagine what it must have been like. We do know that little Nils Gustaf was most tenderly cared for by his paternal aunt Ulrique and her husband Colonel de Frese. Whether his mother ever found time to devote thought and affection to the little boy one can't tell; it is more likely that all her attention was claimed by two more babies that now arrived, and that Nils was left to go very much his own way.

In time, peace was signed and Czar Alexander promised clemency and good posts for the officials of his new Grand Duchy. Refugees and many officers returned, but not Vice-Governor Judge von Schoultz. Such promises did not tempt him to go back; home and possessions were gone, and Sweden seemed safer than a Russian Finland. Besides, he now had much varied and responsible work to do. He became member and treasurer of the Royal Commission for the Liquidation of Field Pay Claims of the Former Finnish Army. He worked out and edited a Project for a New Marching Order for the Army, together with Relevant Establishments and Forms, new travel regulations, and other matters. Yet although he received recognition and gratitude for his conscientious services, his life was not unclouded. Much of his time was spent in drawing up depositions and composing replies to some very serious charges. These related not to himself, but to his father-in-law Major-General Gripenberg.

When disaster has befallen a nation a search for scapegoats always follows. Impelled either by envy or a guilty conscience men swoop like birds of prey on some convenient victim. Hans Henrik Gripenberg had signed the Convention of Seivis and returned to his home in war-ravaged Finland, and it seemed then as if all the grief and shame in Sweden combined to find the very cause of defeat in this Convention, which on 25 March 1809 had been concluded between the Russian army, then invading West Bothnia, and the last remnants of the Finnish forces. The scapegoat chosen was the absent Major-General who, well aware of the probable consequences, accepted full responsibility for 'an act which certainly cast aside a military glory that had ceased to exist, but saved hundreds of lives which would otherwise have been sacrificed in vain'. Gripenberg was summoned to a court-martial to 'declare and substantiate his reasons for subscribing to the Convention'. But although he welcomed this opportunity to defend his reputation, he was in the end denied it, as the Russian authorities would not allow him to leave Finland. He therefore entrusted his son-in-law with the task of preparing and presenting his defence at the court-martial in Stockholm, while continuing to implore permission from the authorities in Turku and St Petersburg to attend it himself.

Judge von Schoultz conducted the defence of the accused with vigour and conviction. The case, which did the accusers little credit, dragged on for two years, until at last Gripenberg was granted permission to appear in it; but by then it was too late. He arrived in Stockholm in the autumn of 1813, and on 25 October he died in his son-in-law's home, at the age of sixty.

In his excellent book about his great-great-uncle, G. A. Gripenberg quotes the old warrior's own words.

With eyes fixed upon honour and duty, calmly and with steadfast loyalty, I have faced death and danger for my King and Country. Secure in the knowledge of this I have raised my head, grown grey in battle, high above misfortune and obloquy, so that I may demand from that country the only reward it can bestow upon me, and one that posterity at least will not deny me: justice: which is to say a reputation without stain.

He was Nils Gustaf's maternal grandfather.

Those whose roots are in Finland find it hard to live happily elsewhere. We know that Judge von Schoultz disliked his career of service in Sweden. Having shared in the dramatic course of the war and played his part in its tragedy, he had now to expend patience and energy in combating 'despicable' forces: 'the biased judgements of enmity, envy, bitterness, ignorance, precipitancy and other contemptible passions'. When Nils Fredrik von Schoultz wrote his memoirs for his children and descendants he was not an old man, but the tone of them is weary and resigned. He expected 'no transition to bliss and joy on this side of the grave'. Yet he is mindful of the thanks he owes a

Benevolent Providence, nor does he doubt 'that in the day of suffering as in the day of gladness his true good is being prepared'. Vice-Governor Judge Nils Fredrik von Schoultz died in Stockholm on 15 January 1816, at the age of forty-nine.

3

School Days with an Idealist

POOR Jeanne was now truly alone: a widow with five children. It is true that her eldest son Fredrik was fifteen at this time, and a promising young officer-cadet, but Nils Gustaf was nine, Carl five, Johanna three and Edvard barely one year old. She could see no alternative but to return to Finland.

Her mother and one unmarried sister were still living at Voipaala, and her youngest brother Sebastian had risen high in the new Grand Duke's favour; but it was to Pori (Björneborg) that Jeanne decided to go, for her brother Odert Gripenberg kept a school for boys there. With him Nils Gustaf and Carl would find affection as well as stimulating guidance.

There is much to tell of Nils Gustaf's uncle, not only because we seem to trace some of his characteristics in his nephew, but because he was a person of unusual and versatile gifts, a very strong-willed and very good man.

At the age of nineteen he took part in the war against the Russians, displayed great courage and was awarded the gold medal for bravery when he was twenty. But when the war was over he had had enough of heroics, and chose another career: that of teacher and educator. After a year of visiting the great educationists of the day – Pestalozzi, Saltzman, von Fellenberg – in whose work he found his own dreams realized, he returned home and with a young kinsman Ulrik von Konow opened a school in Stockholm for 'young sons of honest parents'. But his father insisted that he should return to Finland. If he must be a schoolmaster, he could teach there as well as anywhere else;

indeed it was there, if anywhere, that educational reform was needed. Odert Gripenberg obeyed.

Hardly had he crossed the frontier before benefactors showed a tendency to direct his future. Gustaf Mauritz Armfelt had always taken an interest in the Gripenberg sons, and it was through him that Czar Alexander had heard of the young soldier's unusual character and talents. His Imperial Majesty now summoned Odert to St Petersburg and tried to persuade him to return to military service. He did not succeed. Odert received many offers, but even the post of tutor to the young grand dukes failed to tempt him. Nothing came of it, not only because he could foresee the restrictions that would be imposed on his educational methods, but perhaps even more because of the marked reserve with which H.I.M. viewed the radicalism of a young guards officer who had married purely for love. For this is what Odert Gripenberg had done – and a parish clerk's daughter at that. Nevertheless he received warm encouragement from the Czar, as well as financial aid and the promise of continued favour, and he was able to found a school according to his own ideas.

Gripenberg's Institute, as the school was named, opened in the autumn of 1812 in Hämeenlinna (Tavastehus), and was warmly welcomed by people of standing in the town and district. Yet after only a single term enthusiasm waned. Marvellous results had been expected – and at once. But the boys had learnt nothing in particular; rather less, perhaps, than at their former schools. The new Institute was no good.

It was certainly a very unusual establishment. The pupils were not divided into classes; they all followed the same course of instruction, each at his own speed, though they were examined separately. The masters were young, keen and of recognized ability; some of them were from abroad. The variety of the curriculum is astonishing, but shows emphasis on mathematics and languages. School-hours were long, from seven in the morning to seven at night, though free periods and games were included in the time-table. Gripenberg laid stress on games. Boys must be allowed to laugh and be rowdy, but the important object of the play was to develop quickness of thought and tongue. It was in playing games that one learned how victory is sustained without bumptiousness and defeat without dejection. The boys did indeed receive an excellent education, so that later when they joined the cadet corps in Hamina (Fredrikshamn) they were always among the best candidates.

Unfortunately, as an economist Gripenberg was no more successful than other idealists. He was well aware that fathers in war-torn Finland were poor, and he charged accordingly. Even so the fees seemed too high, and he always took some pupils for nothing, while his foreign teachers demanded big salaries. Ends just would not meet.

Gripenberg moved his school to Pori (Björneborg), where it assumed its permanent form with some forty pupils. But still the scanty coins ran out of the cash box more quickly than they flowed in. Gripenberg now took the school and boys to Sääksmäki, the family home which he had inherited on his father's death; and thus it was that Nils Gustaf enjoyed a few happy years with brothers and sister, cousins and playfellows in beautiful old Voipaala, which had long been a well-loved home for Gripenberg children and grandchildren. Many years later, when the place had passed into other hands, it was described nostalgically in letters and stories:

The big white house stood on the southern slope of the Sääksmäki ride, and the lights from its windows shone protectively over the surrounding land. The children loved the orchard terraces and knew every corner of the fine halls and rooms. On bitter winter mornings and when dusk fell over the manor, crackling fires were lit in the old-fashioned tiled stoves, which were decorated with painted designs in various colours, representing urns, garlands, flowers, birds, griffins and other strange patterns. How often they would admire the fine view from the upper windows! The countryside lay open under God's heaven. The stone church rose above billowing fields of corn, above bays and coves, islets, headlands and shining straits.

There exists a little almanac for 1821, in which the owner Magister Carl Gustaf von Phaler notes the names of boys who arrived at Voipaala after the Christmas holidays. They were officers' sons for the most part, sturdy lads in frieze jackets and dubbed leather boots. No pampered little dandies ever came from the modest homes of army men in the Finland of those days. The master tells how he took the boys to church, and afterwards to the manse to 'taste fresh lemons' which had come from St Petersburg. He taught them to plant potatoes and to fish, and let them toboggan down the slopes while the wind whistled round their ears. They were allowed to listen to violin and piano when the Gripenbergs made music; and some of them at least were infected by Odert's passion for inventions when he demonstrated his ingenious seed-sowing machine, which he never ceased to improve.

The almanac records walks, expeditions and April Fooleries, when the pupils 'hurried off to see a flying fish!' There was no humdrum routine about these boys' schooling. Most of them did well in after life, and were gentlemen in the best sense of the word. They were not living in the wilderness, after all: they visited neighbouring manors and met guests who came from far away. The most notable of these while the school was housed at Voipaala was the Czar himself.

From the founding of the school he had shown a continuing interest in its fortunes, and in the course of his official progress through the country in 1819 he honoured it with a visit, which is described in Carl von Schoultz's memoirs.

Carl was then only eight years old, but he well recalled how, after a couple of hours' lessons at which the Czar was present, all the boys paraded before their illustrious patron. Carl also betrays a minor calamity which must certainly have remained a secret in the family, to be mentioned only with the utmost discretion.

On arriving, the Czar, conducted by my younger uncle Sebastian who was in attendance during his journeys through Finland, hastened up to my grandmother and seated himself beside her on a small sofa. Grandmother, unaware that H.I.M. had left in advance of his numerous suite and had already arrived, said to her son in Swedish: 'Request the Russian general to take a chair: the place on the sofa must be kept free for the Czar, whom we expect within a few minutes. The general is crumpling the cover.'

'What is your mother saying?' asked the Czar, turning to his gentleman in waiting. 'I can see that something is troubling her.' The explanation was given, whereupon H.I.M. caused the presentation to be made. He kissed grandmother's hands and begged her acceptance of a precious piece of jewellery, which he then handed to her as a memento of their first meeting.

Such was the shock of the old lady's surprise that when, after some refreshment, the Czar took his leave and she rose from the sofa, a large wet patch was to be seen where she had sat and upon the back of her gown.

The Czar's visit certainly shed glory upon the school and boys, but the ringing gold so greatly needed weighed little, and did not go far when it arrived. Strongly advised by General Thesleff, H.I.M. gave his gracious approval to the removing of the Institute to Hamina (Fredrikshamn) in the autumn of 1821, where it continued to function as preparatory school for the cadet-corps.

Odert Gripenberg had worries and anxieties all his life. He followed his chosen star with determination and nothing could deflect him from his course, but he drove people wild with his obstinacy. Armfelt, who wished him all the good in the world, had been unable to persuade the young man to rejoin the army; later he failed equally in inducing him to transfer his school to Viipuri (Viborg). Finally he allowed his exasperation to boil

over in a letter to Governor G. F. Stjernvall: '... everlasting
projects, combined with stubborn insistence on unsuitable
methods, which together result in a mass of contradictions impossible to carry into effect...'

But Professor J. J. Nordström, a friend of Gripenberg's who
knew all his vicissitudes, wrote, deeply moved at his death, that
'one seldom meets a man of so unprejudiced a mind, so lofty a
character or a heart so susceptible to the greatness in humanity.
A noble man'.

Jacob Grot, professor of Russian, looking at him with the
eye of a foreigner, saw him when he was blind and poor, and
speaks of 'this exceptional man, whose noble face shone with
serenity and joy'. Grot was convinced that 'there are few people
in the world to compare in greatness of soul with Gripenberg'.

It was with this uncle and in the world he created round him
that Nils Gustaf lived for five important years, from nine to
fourteen. How deeply was the boy affected by this masculine
world, based on the principles of freedom and self-discipline?
Freedom suited him well; the rest he cannot have taken much
to heart. From his father he inherited an enthusiasm for music
and mathematics, and these talents were well cultivated here.
From no one, it seems, did he acquire the art of dealing with
worldly realities.

4

The Family in Stockholm

WHEN Odert Gripenberg and his pupils moved from Voipaala to Hamina, his sister Jeanne and her children also left. The widow may have begun to weary of life in Finland, where everything seemed transient and precarious, and once more she decided to go to Sweden. In the late summer of 1821 she moved to Stockholm, where her eldest son – good, reliable, pleasant Fredrik – had followed his appointed path from the Royal Military Academy, Karlberg, to the Göta Artillery, and was now a promising young officer. It was now high time for Nils Gustaf to qualify for the military academy; and this he duly did. On 20 December 1821 he was made sergeant in the Svea Regiment of Artillery, and on 3 December 1823 was promoted to second lieutenant. That is all we know of the young man at this period of his life.

However, among his talented family there was one observer who in his old age wrote down his recollections of a varied life. This was his brother Carl, whose memoirs delighted and scandalized later generations, and who evidently had an excellent memory for what he heard and saw. He had a taste for momentous events as well as for picturesque detail; yet most often his own self-important figure takes the centre of the stage, overshadowing everything and everyone else. Never does he describe either his mother or his brothers and sister: they are elbowed into the background of scenes which they should have dominated. Their lives and fortunes concerned him not at all, and only once does he mention his brother Nils Gustaf.

Fru von Schoultz settled down in a house of her own in Stockholm: a handsome property with a large garden in the southern district. There life seems to have passed contentedly and securely for some years. In his memoirs Carl writes cheerfully enough of that hospitable home, yet with no little self-pity for the chief character, so hardly done by, so left out. For while the other brothers, including Edvard, the youngest, were all following the family's military tradition, he, Carl, suffered the ignominy of an apprenticeship to one Söderberg, a wholesale merchant. Admittedly he is careful to mention that the old gentleman was not just any little shopkeeper, but a highly respected man, father-in-law of R. von Kraemer, later governor of the province of Uppsala. He showed his young apprentice consideration and kindness.

Carl's assertion that he was sacrificing himself for the sake of the family income is unconvincing; one suspects that he was merely dodging military studies and drill. Yet he resentfully parades his feelings of being odd man out.

. . . when I came home after a long day spent among herring-barrels and dusty grain, tired, cold and dirty, I sometimes heard as I entered the hall the sound of gay voices from the inner rooms. A whole party of old and young friends of the family, amused and entertained by the talents of my sister and of my two elder brothers, had spent the evening in my hospitable and friendly home, in songs, recitations, charades, *bouts-rimés* . . . and dancing, which were customary diversions in a cultured home of that day. I did not always submit to the fatigue of changing my clothes, but preferred to withdraw quietly and unobserved to the room I shared with Edvard, to take a little refreshment and then go to bed. On such occasions sleep was sometimes long delayed by my reflections upon the diversity of the lives led by members of the same family . . .

Yet the working day did not always end so peaceably. Once when having come home and changed I entered the room, a young officer called out 'Ha, here comes the Councillor of Commerce! How are things on 'Change today?' 'I don't know,' I replied, somewhat offended, 'but I did hear that there'd been a sharp fall in subalterns.' There was laughter, but I seemed to feel a stab at my heart, and when I went to bed I wept at my innate malice, and would have liked to embrace the young fellow and discharge some of his little debts out of my salary.

Was that insolent young fellow Nils Gustaf? And were his debts still only trifling?

But it is when Carl tells of their summer merrymakings that we seem to sense the lightheartedness of one of Bellman's melodies: 'Excursions from our home to the Djurgården parks and royal residences. We would hire one of the expensive rowing-boats with its dreadful great oarswomen. We took umbrellas with us and a well-stocked picnic-basket, and hoped for good weather. When it rained and blew the whole affair was disagreeable and costly, but most often we had great fun.'

The boys had a pretty young sister. Professor Otto Andersson has described her brilliant but tragically brief career as a singer, in a well-documented and interesting biography. It is he rather than her brother Carl that we have to thank for many details in this present account. When she was still quite small, says Professor Andersson, Johanna von Schoultz delighted everyone with her silvery treble; and now the attractive Fröken von Schoultz with her beautiful singing-voice was beginning to be talked of more and more widely. An unusually fine soprano, people said. Her two elder brothers were known for their good voices; Fredrik was considered the best tenor in Stockholm. There was always music at the von Schoultz's, though of this Carl chooses to say nothing.

Nevertheless it seems they went to the play and the opera, heard great artists and were present at the spectacular fire in *Dramatiska teatern*. They were among the crowds in Djurgården park when Queen Désirée and the beautiful young Princess Josephine arrived in a warship and were received by King Karl Johan.

Those charming young officers, Fredrik and Nils Gustaf, were to be seen everywhere. They were invited by the Crown Prince to balls and musical soirées; they distinguished themselves in elegant mazurkas à la St Petersburg and performed languishing duets. Fredrik sang with His Royal Highness himself.

Then one evening in the winter of 1827, Fredrik mentioned that, at a court ball the night before, the Crown Prince had engaged him in a long conversation.

His Royal Highness had heard from several people that young Fröken von Schoultz had been endowed with a wonderfully fine and powerful soprano voice, and he thought her family ought not to allow unreasonable prejudice to hinder the training of this glorious natural gift. She should take lessons for a few months from Craelius, and then from the celebrated Professor Siboni of Copenhagen. If financial help were needed, the Prince would gladly furnish it.

Sensation. The brothers of course painted a brilliant future for their sister, in the glow of footlights, amid storms of applause and showers of gold. What may little Johanna have thought of it?

When one is fourteen, tenderly loved by four brothers, without ever having caught more than a glimpse of the cares of the world, what can one believe except that everything will come to pass as foretold, and that one was born just to sing and to be cherished by more and more kind people? But Fru Jeanne felt no such rapture. It was months before any coaxing could quell her indignation at the mere thought of her daughter 'treading the boards'.

But this was not at all the intention, protested Fredrik. As a concert-singer a well-born lady might very well make a famous name for herself, and amass a considerable fortune. Several friends of the family, 'highly respected ladies such as Countess Sparre, née Montgomery . . . and many more were of the Prince's opinion'. Moreover – useless to deny it – money had its attractions.

One senses something alien, a trace of exile, in the attitude and conversation of the von Schoultz family. A happiness long lost glowed from the past. Sweden was not their home; it was also a place where it was awkward not to be rich. Here one had to have money to maintain one's proper position in society. Renewed discussion resulted in the summoning of old Craelius; the singing lessons began and the future took on a radiance undimmed by any hint of approaching storms.

All went well. Johanna sang like a bird, easily and gaily. 'Her voice increased in power, and her performance in artistry and charm,' wrote Carl. 'The crowning tribute was paid on 3 May 1828, at a concert given before a packed audience in Ladugårds-land Church, in the presence of the whole Royal Family. During the interval the royal personages were graciously pleased to enter the sacristy, to congratulate the young singer upon her present success and to wish her well for the future, both at home and abroad. Surrounded by the orchestra of the Harmonic Asso-ciation, Johanna took her place on a spacious platform which had been especially erected for the occasion, and to which she was led by her eldest brother wearing full regi-mentals.'

Let us hope that Nils Gustaf, too, was sunning himself in these splendours, for once more the hour of dispersal was at hand, and this time for good. Johanna's studies were to continue first with Siboni in Copenhagen, and later with more eminent masters in Italy and Paris.

A young lady could not travel alone, and the family very properly agreed that Johanna should be accompanied by her mother, 'for the security and comfort of domestic life'. Yet even two ladies could not travel without masculine protection, 'having regard to the singing-lessons and to greatly extended social intercourse in the future'. This gave brother Carl the chance of his life. The two elder brothers could not interrupt their army career, while Edvard was a boy of only thirteen, destined for the military academy of Karlberg; so Carl was chosen to be the ladies' escort. Besides, as he smugly observes, 'as all my family agreed, in me were united an exceptional knowledge of languages and of the usages of polite society, with strict moral principles and exemplary conduct.'

A sly hint that the same could not be said of every member of the family?

Carl says nothing of his financial ability or thrift, and we are bound in honesty to note that the seventeen-year-old guide and keeper of the purse made full use of his opportunities. Lamentations in his diary over his interrupted career and abandoned studies are not convincing; he was delighted to turn his back on the salt herrings. 'Of the large fortune amassed in the capital cities, two hundred thousand riksdaler were to fall to my share, to secure my future livelihood,' notes the memoir-writer. Uncle Sebastian in Finland approved of the plans, and contributed a few thousand riksdaler towards travelling-expenses.

When Jeanne and her two children drove down to Copenhagen, in the autumn of 1828, it was as if they were on a delightful excursion to visit close friends. They broke their journey twice, for a couple of days with Countess of Wetterstedt at Finspång, the second time to visit Fredrik's fiancée, Pauline Cronhjelm. In Malmö they were received most hospitably by the Posse family and found time to attend the splendid ball of the order of Amaranth. Copenhagen was equally enchanting. At a big reception there, held by the Swedish minister, Johanna and Carl were presented to the Royal Family, on which occasion the King was pleased to observe to his host: 'Those two young people might have been born and bred at court.' Johanna sang and was warmly applauded, and won a valuable piece of jewellery in a raffle.

After some months of diligent study by Johanna, the trio returned to Stockholm to make their final farewells. But first came a number of successful recitals in Sweden, Norway and

Denmark, and then in Sweden again. When they finally left, in the spring of 1832, they travelled via St Petersburg, Finland (for more farewells), Lübeck and thence to Italy, all in the same grand style, with royal letters of introduction in their luggage and a purse well-filled with royal gold.

5

Polish Adventure

It seemed that the von Schoultz family had dispersed for ever when they said goodbye before Johanna's departure for Copenhagen. Once the rumble of the travelling-carriage wheels had died away, a strange silence descended on the three brothers in the Stockholm house. Did they remain there? Fredrik was an officer in the Guards, and betrothed to Fröken Pauline Cronhjelm. Edvard was at Karlberg Military Academy. But Nils Gustaf? He spent some holidays with Ulrique de Frese, his aunt and godmother, who during the hard post-war years had been a true foster-mother to him. Beyond this we know almost nothing of the boys' lives and doings during the years that followed. No doubt they led a more solitary existence and a meagre one, on their subalterns' pay – and a second lieutenant is not slow to spend what little he has. And that was all Nils Gustaf had to live on. A letter has been found telling us that he was expected in Finland for Christmas 1830: the writer says that she 'will extract a promise from him to spend Christmas here'.

But later there were agitated whispers in the family about gambling-debts and other shady affairs during this period: things that were never made clear and which cast their shadows far into the future. All trace of them seems to have been swept away. His military conduct was good, and on 29 May 1829 he passed the gunner officers' examination at Marieberg, at which 'His Royal Highness the Crown Prince graciously presided.' He continued in the service until suddenly, in October 1830, he applied for his discharge.

His colonel forwarded the application for His Majesty's gracious consideration. The reply came in an autographed letter, and 'open letter of discharge from military service', dated 13 November 1830, and with the customary handsome peroration testifying to 'Our Gracious Satisfaction with his past loyal service and good conduct'.

After his discharge Nils Gustaf stayed on as lay assessor at the regimental court-martial, and as invigilator at the junior officers' examination. Thus the regiment can have found no fault to find with him; quite the reverse. But after that we hear no more.

Did he feel restless and rootless? Was life dull, now that the house was empty? When his mother was there, relations and friends would call in from Finland with news – now cheerful, now alarming. At times their tidings would melt all hearts with nostalgia for their own country; at others they brought worry with the knowledge of the secret dread – the threat of bondage – weighing upon those who had remained. Life in that safe house on the outskirts of Stockholm, had been a typical life of *emigrés*, of *ci-devants*, with drawing-room politics and intrigues. No wonder, then, if it now seemed drab, and Sweden small.

Did Nils Gustaf feel overshadowed by Fredrik, that elegant, engaging guards officer who had the entrée everywhere? Nils was one of those 'penniless younger sons' so eloquently hailed by Eirik Hornborg as 'soldiers of fortune, ever ready for battle, ever hungering for pay and plunder'. 'A turbulent, dangerous element,' he calls them, poised for bold enterprises and break-neck exploits. *Les fils cadets.* Certainly Nils Gustaf was of their company.

He had heard how his great-grandfather had crossed Europe many times on errands for Charles XII of Sweden, from Turkey to Norway. His grandfather had been commandant of Svartholm. His mother's brother Gustaf had marched with Napoleon against Alexander, and fell at Borodino.

Surely, even now, there must be a little war somewhere, where a brave man could win glory, if not gold?

The truth was much sterner. From Poland rumours were coming in of growing oppression, and of fierce resistance. Students and cadets in Warsaw had raised the standard of rebellion and summoned the defenders of freedom – such as there were – to do battle against the oppressor. It was known that the new Czar was the sworn foe to all liberty, and that he held the fate of Poland – and of Finland too – in his iron grasp. How could a von Schoultz, born in Finland and with the Polish Czultzecky blood in his veins, stand idly by while freedom itself was perishing! Especially now on hearing that another von Schoultz – one of those who had stayed in Finland, cousin Constantin Nils Lorentz von Schoultz of the Finnish Regiment of Russian Lifeguards – had been sent to Poland to crush the rebellion.

'The crime of a Schoultz shall be atoned for by a Schoultz.'

Nils Gustaf disappeared. He left for Poland – with Frans Hartman, a fellow ex-officer from the regiment – in the greatest secrecy; for the Swedish government refused to compromise itself in the eyes of the powerful and easily-provoked Czar, and had curtly rejected all appeals made to it by Polish patriots. In Sweden, as in Finland, pro-Polish sympathies could be aired only behind closed doors. Even the most influential people, whose names commanded international admiration and respect, preferred that their affairs in the Poland of 1831 should not be needlessly discussed. Therefore very little is known, and hardly anything with certainty, of their participation in the Polish struggle for freedom.

But besides Schoultz and Hartman there were some young men, not content with drinking toasts and making fiery speeches, who were fortunate enough to obtain official sanction for their enterprise.

An appeal for voluntary help in military hospitals was circulated throughout Sweden with official consent. Three young physicians in Lund responded to this appeal and sailed for Königsberg. One of them, Dr S. J. Stille, afterwards gave a vivid description of the break-neck journey to Warsaw and of his six-months' work as field-surgeon: 'Assistant Physician to Camp I'. It is from this account that we gain some notion of Nils Gustaf's activities.

The three men from Lund left Sweden on 6 May 1831 and reached Warsaw on 10 June. 'The sun was setting in a crimson sky as if it were sinking in blood: a prefiguration of Poland's, of Warsaw's, fate,' wrote Stille. The Swedish doctors had travelled through country still untouched by the ravages of war, and Dr Stille admired the lush fertility of the fields and the cheerfulness of the people. Warsaw was impressive in its beauty and richness. The hospitals that he saw and worked in were excellent, being well-supplied with lint, bandages, compresses and so forth. Physicians from almost every country flocked to the aid of their Polish colleagues, for the casualty-rate among doctors was incredibly high. Vacancies were continually occurring, partly because of death in battle, or cholera, partly because 'the Cossacks received ducats for every doctor they captured alive for the Russian army.'

Finally Dr Stille describes his encounter with a young soldier, 'one of the many eager champions of liberty who had rallied to the support of the Polish patriots'.

On 2 August [1831] I was going on sick-rounds in my section, when a person quite unknown to me approached and asked me in French whether any Swedish physicians were attached to this hospital. When I replied that there were three, of whom I was one, he cried out most joyfully in the Swedish language, as he embraced me: 'Then I have come to the right place! My name is S—,' he continued. 'I am Swedish and am at present serving as a Volunteer with the second Uhlan Regiment.' I can recall no occasion when I have been more joyfully surprised, and we at once formed a fraternal alliance, both as compatriots and friends.

I then accompanied him to the Hôtel de Wilna, where he was quartered. He told me that Skrzynecki, the Commander-in-Chief, had enrolled him into the Polish Army, and had told him that there would soon be a battle, and that he – S— – should have the first officer's vacancy that occurred. S— then begged to be accepted as a Volunteer, saying that having never been in the field he felt unworthy to command seasoned and victorious Soldiers: 'Let me first become a brave fighter, and then, should I deserve it, the General may honour me with promotion.' Skrzynecki replied with a kindly smile: 'One can hear that you're a Swede, and it shall be as you wish. From this moment you are a Volunteer with the second Uhlan Regiment, the finest cavalry in the Polish Army, and there you will find your best opportunity to show your courage.'

Skrzynecki wanted S— to remain for two or three days in Warsaw so as to procure a uniform, etc; but the latter, dreading lest some conflict should arise meanwhile in which he would be unable to take part, undertook to equip himself.

Therefore, he handed over to me, as being better acquainted with the neighbourhood, some civilian clothes which I sold to a Jew. With this money S— bought a set of Uhlan regimentals which were far from smart and would not have done for the ball-room, but which would have been serviceable nevertheless had they not split upon his first attempt to mount his horse.

The young doctor must have been as light-hearted as the Swedish Uhlan, for he continues his description of his friend in the same lively fashion:

He was a Swede of a past age, courageous and bold to foolhardiness; the joy beaming from his eyes as he prepared for battle was so genuine as to hearten all those who came in company with him, and as to persuade his comrades that there could be no peril where S— was absent.

When we parted, I said something of our Country's Honour and Poland's Liberty, whereupon he drew his sabre, on which he had caused to be engraved:

The steel of Sweden bites
And we shall prove it true.
Give way, ye Muscovites,
Lay on, bold Boys in Blue!

and brandished it over his head, crying, 'Be assured that I shall charge into the thick of the enemy for Sweden's honour and Polish freedom.' He then hastened away to take his part in the sacred fight for liberty, truth and justice.

People persuaded themselves that victory was assured, while in reality calumny and envy, like moles, had so successfully undermined the leadership, that General Skrzynecki, faultless in the eyes of the patriots and adored by the whole nation, was removed from his command and replaced by a fortune-hunter who sold the country to the enemy. Stille gives horrifying pictures of the chaos and bloodshed which he witnessed in Warsaw before the retreating army marched into the city.

'The joy with which everyone, save the rioters, beheld the Polish Army entering the city and bivouacking in the streets is scarcely to be imagined,' he writes. The army had been in danger of being cut off from Warsaw by the Russians, and to cover their retreat had set fire to the village of Wola, on the outskirts. They now pitched camp in streets and squares. 'The artillery kept their cannon loaded and their matches alight, and the cavalry their mounts saddled, in order to attack the mob at the first sign of tumult. But this evening was as merry as the previous one had been ghastly. Camp fires blazed in the streets and the soldiers sat about them in groups, cleaning their rifles amid song and laughter.'

In the course of these tense, dramatic days the doctor met his gallant countryman again. He found him

in Sigmund's Square amid a crowd of companions by whom he was regarded as a Lion of the North: a title which that tried and tested corps would never have bestowed upon anyone unworthy of it.

My friends and I spent some convivial hours with the young firebrand, who described with delight the valour of the Poles in the action. He told us among other things that when ordered to cover the guns, they often played cards and smoked tobacco in a rain of shot, and whenever the enemy let fly a powerful volley they shouted '*Vivat!*' and sang: '*Noch is Polen nicht verloren*'.

S— was gaiety itself, and longed for the day when Russia would attempt an assault. . . . His only complaint was of his horse, which he said was stumble-footed; but he consoled himself directly, being persuaded that he would soon acquire a better one from the Russian cavalry, or from the Cossacks.

He had bivouacked ever since entering the Polish service, and had not had his clothes off once in all that time; one must admire a body that can maintain good health in so many unfavourable circumstances.

One of his narratives gave us little pleasure, however, chiefly because we were less assured than he that liberty would triumph. He told us that the Russians hanged all students and cadets they came upon, without mercy. We had heard this from the cadets themselves, and that the reason for it was that these Corps were the first to begin the revolt in Warsaw; but when he went on to say that according to rumour the Russians also hanged every tenth foreigner who had been in Polish service and was taken prisoner, he was telling us something new and not altogether agreeable . . .

These few hours soon passed and the Swedish Uhlan hastened back to rejoin his comrades in arms. Before he left he begged that if we arrived safe home again and he did not, we should greet his fellow-countrymen from him and say: 'S— fell as a soldier; they never hanged him.'

A grim jest, with an undying echo!

This was the last time that Stille encountered his bombastic friend, for after that their paths diverged. The gallant Uhlan is said to have been awarded the Polish cross of valour; he then vanished into Galicia or Prussia.

If this was not Nils Gustaf von Schoultz it must have been his double: here was the same manner, the same magnetic personality. Most convincing of all: wherever von Schoultz went in the years that followed, he was spoken of and his behaviour described in terms identical to these.

All we know for certain is that Nils Gustaf went to Poland, plunged headlong into the battle for freedom and took part in the defence of Warsaw. He was captured by the Russians, and managed to escape with eighteen of his fellows.

Wounded, ragged and hungry he made his way through Europe to France. There Louis-Philippe had recently united the remnants of foreign regiments that had served in France into La Légion Etrangère. This was formed after the July revolution with the object, it was said, of restraining the vagabonds and turbulent spirits who were still swarming about France and the rest of Europe, ripe for any mischief. Nils Gustaf was of this order, and he was not alone: many another *fils cadet* had fallen among bad company, at the Paris barricades.

The Legion was sent to Africa, and Nils with it. We have no details of his stay there, though some hideous scenes can be glimpsed as it were by lightning flashes. He said afterwards that he had taken part in the massacre of a whole tribe of Arabs. When in the hush of death after the battle he walked over the ground and saw helpless old men, women and children lying piled on top of each other, he would have given his life to have had no share in it.

He had had enough. He had to get out. In the spring of 1832 he succeeded, and arrived safely in Marseilles. From there he went on to Italy and to Florence, to seek out his mother, sister and brother.

Nils Gustaf arrived in Florence on 2 March 1833.

6

Foreigners in Florence

'A MOST delightful day,' wrote a young lady, sitting by candle-light in the blue drawing room of the Casa Nobili. She had been out driving with her friends to La Cascine, to enjoy the spring in that wonderful park beside the Arno. While the rest of the party strolled on along the river bank she remained in the carriage, dreaming. She could have had no premonition what her fate was entering the city, for then she would never have written 'a most delightful day'.

By this time Jeanne von Schoultz and her two children were well established in Florence. Their arrival in the summer of 1832 had been heralded by royal messages from the north, and they soon found a beautifully furnished suite of rooms in Casa Credi, a large house near Porta Croce occupied by the distinguished old Swedish minister Lagersvärd. In the garden at the back was the dwelling of the learned chamberlain and librarian of the Biblioteca Pitti, who was also the Swedish consul (later to be Count Gråberg of Hemsö), and his two talented daughters. The von Schoultz ladies lost no time in calling upon Julie, sister of the Queen of Sweden. This amiable lady had once worn but soon lost the crown of Spain, and now lived in the fading glory of the great Napoleonic days, in the society of skittish princesses, unemployed monarchs and ineffectual princes. The newcomers were expected and eagerly awaited by her, as messengers from the bleak north to which fate had banished Désirée Bernadotte. To her countless questions they were able to return replies that were both welcome and truthful; they could describe how beloved the queen was by all, and how her husband was admired and almost worshipped by his subjects.

It was hardly to be wondered at, then, that all doors should be thrown open to the newcomers, and that they should be welcomed as rightful members of that exclusive little world from which all everyday cares were excluded, and where genius and taste seemed to dwell in harmony with *dolce far niente*. But Johanna began her studies without delay, and worked hard. Monsieur Charles had now to set about his duties as escort, and he chaperoned Johanna more or less patiently during her long lessons with different teachers. What 'studies of my own' he pursued does not appear from the diary, but he certainly flitted like a fish in water through this new and glittering world.

One of Johanna's teachers was the renowned old Velluti, who was immediately interested in and attracted by his new pupil. He praised the beauty and range of her voice, and her musical maturity, and he hastened to introduce her to the best musical circles in Florence. In this way Johanna met Madame de Valabrègue, who was the divine Angelica Catalani.

They may have met before. During Catalani's visit to Sweden she wrote her name and a few kind words in an album belonging to Pauline Cronhjelm, Johanna's sister-in-law to be. In Florence their friendship developed.

Every Sunday evening a large party gathered in the salon of Mme de Valabrègue's magnificent villa, La Loggia, above Florence, to make music and listen to it. These were memorable evenings, for the hostess was not only a great artist, adored and admired by her contemporaries, but an enchanting person, intelligent, warm-hearted and full of temperament. Where she was present, the rhythm of life became a dance of the gods, and people who met at her house were soon friends. In this way Johanna and Carl met two pretty girls at La Loggia – two 'chestnut-blonde' Scots who at once aroused their curiosity.

They were sisters; their names were Ann and Mary Campbell,

and they had lived in Florence for about a year. They came of a good Highland family; their father Alexander Campbell was son of the legendary John Campbell of The Bank (the Royal Bank of Scotland), a rich and respected man; but as Alexander was the seventh son and the last of fourteen children, it seemed best for the young man to seek his fortune abroad. After making the *petit tour* in France he sailed for India in the service of the East India Company. He did well, and was soon accounted one of the 'the most respectable' members of European society in Calcutta.

The girls' mother was a Frazer of the proud Jacobite Frazers of Fairfield. She too had 'set forth on her adventures', as her father described her journey to London with her two sisters. But the journey was in every way suitable. Ann, the youngest, had married a cousin, Captain Andrew Frazer, and with her newborn daughter was to accompany her husband to India. The sisters sailed with them as far as London, to mitigate the pain of parting, and also to see something of the world beyond their wild native hills.

In London Elisabeth was captured by a young painter who was already well-known and successful, Thomas Phillips R.A. She married him and went to live in his beautiful little house in Hanover Square. She was to live in this home all her life, and it became the one fixed point in the fluctuating existence of her sisters and nieces.

Mary the third sister decided at once not to return to a now unendurably dismal Scotland, and she accompanied her sister and brother-in-law to India. There she landed in the arms of an agreeable and reassuringly rich compatriot, and in 1811 became Mrs Alexander Campbell. It was in their large bungalow in The Gardens, the European residential area outside Calcutta, that Ann Cordelia was born. 'My goldilocks is really a beautiful baby,' wrote her rapturous father to his family in Scotland.

For four years she lived in India, cherished by her gentle

ayah and her faithful dark-skinned bearer Ruupan. At her parents' wish she learned Hindustani from them, for she might well spend her whole life in India. Later her mother began to speak English with her, but it was not until she was on the long voyage to England that she learned the beautiful English on which she was afterwards so often complimented. She quite forgot the Hindustani that she had been taught with such care and foresight and spoke so prettily, but preserved hazy memories of those happy childhood years, like pictures of a paradise for ever lost.

No one knows how much Ann remembered of that fearful voyage from Calcutta round the Cape to London. In September 1818 she joined her four little cousins in Aunt Elisabeth's and Uncle Thomas's spacious nursery: two of them were Mary and Scott Phillips, the children of the house, and the others were Susan and Henrietta Frazer whom Ann had played with at home in India. They were to be like well-loved sisters and brother to her for the rest of her life.

Ann never saw her father again. He died in 1821, and Mary Campbell returned with Ann's little sister Mary, and later took Ann and the two Frazer nieces to Edinburgh. Aunt Elisabeth had given her five girls (two daughters of her own and three adopted) an impeccable upbringing – truly Victorian long before Victoria – based on principles of neatness, dutiful behaviour, seriousness, self-control, and with 'noble thoughts and an agreeable manner'. But from the outset there had been solid instruction too, under good teachers, as well as needlework and drawing. It was a real school for life, and Ann bore the impress of it to her dying day. Mary's attitude was easier; her children had books of a different kind, as well as music and dancing.

When Ann was thirteen Mary took her party of girls over to Ghent, feeling it to be high time for her daughters – and even more urgent for Susan and Henrietta, who would soon be entering the grown-up world in India – to receive a continental polish to their education. She was accompanied by an unmarried sister-in-law, the kindly Christie Campbell, who also brought with her a girl confided to her care. After two years, when the charming Frazer girls were thought perfect enough to sail for India, the rest of the party went on to Paris. Other members of the family began to feel that it was time these roving ladies returned; but they continued south to Orléans, Lyons, Marseille and, via Genoa and Leghorn, to Florence. They may have dreamt of Rome, but that dream never came true. During the years abroad Christie Campbell had greatly aged and funds were slowly shrinking. Yet to have reached Florence was enough for Ann. She had read about Italy and about Dante and Beatrice one summer when she was eleven years old. Now she was eighteen, and life could begin.

Johanna von Schoultz felt the same, and from their first meeting the girls were friends. Ann Campbell too was very musical; she played the piano and guitar and sang in a soft, deep voice. Her young sister Mary was only fourteen and a real little whirlwind, with no particularly admirable qualities beyond a quick tongue and dancing feet. During the spring of 1833 Mademoiselle Johanna and Monsieur Charles appear over and over again in Ann's journal, and are joined there one fine day by their brother Monsieur Nicolas.

This is how the story was told to me as a child.

Spring had come to Florence, that marvellous city among the Tuscan hills. Grass and vines began to weave shimmering greenery over slopes that had lain brown and silent all the winter. Larks soared, and the river flowed rippling and glittering under its peerless bridges. The town was filled with the clamour of carnival; merry-makers thronged the squares and streamed in procession through the narrow streets. The windows of the old palaces stood open, and from them the rich and noble citizens had hung out their splendours in the city's honour.

Madame von Schoultz and her daughter, that attractive young

singer from the north, were entertaining a large party in their rooms at Casa Credi, near Porta Croce. People jostled at the windows, joking and laughing and pointing out grotesque masks in the crowd below.

Look, there went a monk, rolling a huge wine-cask in front of him – but he was no true monk: there were curls on his forehead. And from under that black domino what a delicate little hand had just blown a kiss. Its owner must surely live in a palazzo, and had escaped for only a little while from a strict mother. And here came a brigand – the one gazing up at them. He looked horribly realistic, but superb all the same.

At that moment the sun and the din must have been too much for Mme de Schoultz, for she nearly fainted. Her young guests hurried to her with smelling salts and good advice. Carl, having helped his mother to her room, slipped away unnoticed.

He rushed downstairs and out into the milling crowds to look for the ragged brigand whom for a moment they had seen pass by. He found him: it was his brother Nils Gustaf.

Carl says nothing in his memoirs about this encounter, but there must have been more pain and reproach in it than joy. How and when had Nils left Sweden? Where had he been? Could he answer all their questions? How grievous was the meeting of mother and son?

Alas, all was not sunshine at Casa Credi. Johanna was more delicate than had been realized – or admitted. Winter in Florence was worse than winter at home, and the heat of summer was appalling. As often as not she had a cough or a sore throat. The truth had begun to dawn on Johanna herself – the cold hard reality that lurked behind the golden visions that she had been tricked into believing. She dreaded appearing before a strange audience; the carefree daytime life turned in the darkness to nightmare. Poor gentle Johanna, poor anxious mother.

And now suddenly there appears this desperado of a son,

fresh from unknown, dubious escapades. How was his presence to be explained? What plans had he for the future? He refused to answer questions, and seemed to want nothing but to be taken care of, to rest and get his breath back.

But his mother had dealt with worse predicaments in her day. For the moment all that mattered was to make the young man presentable and launch him into society. And indeed, within a few days Mme de Schoultz introduced her second son, the young officer who, on his way home from some military expedition, was able to rejoin his family for a time and enjoy the Italian spring. He had graceful manners and an engaging personality, like M. Charles, or even more so. There was an air of mystery about him, a Byronic touch. He was not as tall as Charles, but strong and well-built. His grave face was browned by the African sun and worn by the camp-sickness that still periodically attacked him. He inspired both apprehension and confidence.

It was a radiant spring. A whim of fate had brought together these young people from the bleak, chilly lands of the north in this enchanting world of warmth and beauty. Among all the famous and brilliant people whom Johanna had met here, why should she have attached herself in particular to naïve, trusting Ann Campbell? It was to her and her mischievous little sister Mary that sprightly M. Charles also turned, to boast of his adventures in high society. Yet when all was said, it was music that directed the action in this *commedia dell' arte*. Il capitano was now on stage.

One evening Nils Gustaf went with the rest of his family to Mme Catalani's. We know that it was 10 March 1833, for it is under that date that Ann Campbell wrote in her journal:

... This evening was as rainy and disagreeable as the last and very cold, but we had fixed with Miss de Schoultz to go to Madame Valabrègue's tonight ... and having reached the door of the Villa were kept waiting in silence and darkness, and at last found that

Madame was just going to bed, but when she heard that [we] were there had caused the candles and fire to be lighted immediately. She kissed us all when we came in and laughed immoderately at poor Mme Vivier [her daughter] having to put on her clothes again. She had received a levée in the morning, and said she was going to bed toute triste et toute seule when we were announced and she was very glad to see us. She hopped off to put on another cap, and then we talked till Madame de Schoultz, her daughter and her two sons arrived. She is an immense woman both in height and breadth, but notwithstanding that, and the snuff she takes, she is quite a fine *lady*, in manners and appearance. Her children resemble her very much. She has a pension from the Swedish government, but it does not permit her to live in her own country in the manner to which she has been accustomed, so that is the reason her daughter is to make use of her voice.

Two lines have been very vigorously scratched out at this point, whether then or later, and Ann continues:

She has two sons in the army, the third remains with them as their protector and travelling-companion. After tea, Miss de Schoultz played us some beautiful variations on Weber's last piece, and then she placed herself on her knees before Madame Catalani who came immediately, and first sung the prayer out of Anna Bolena; hers is the voice to my taste the most beautiful I have ever heard, and her shakes, runs and cadences are something ethereal. Then to look at her, she seems an angel descended from the spheres, or an inspired creature quite removed from earth. When she has once begun there is no difficulty in getting her to proceed, and she sang an anthem, a bolero, the duet of the Gazza Ladra, *Ebbene per mia Memoria,* and a beautiful piece of Rossini's which she sounded through her lips like the tones of a clarinet. Then she is so sweet, so unaffected. She is a delightful creature. When she sings her mouth wears a natural smile of the most lovely expression, and her whole face seems beaming with poetry. So, I thought, I am now actually listening to the voice and sitting by the woman I have heard of since childhood.

Later they danced:

Mlle de Schoultz and her brother Ni— [Ann attempted to write his name, but evidently found it difficult, and scratched it out] showed us how the Mazourka is danced in Russia, very different and much prettier than the Italianized Mazourka danced here. It was now becoming late, and after taking some lemonade, and thanking and bidding adieu to the kind mistress of the mansion, we reached home at past twelve.

This is the first mention of the man with the odd name in Ann's diary, and it is some time before we come upon another. To begin with she wrote 'M. Nicolas', then 'Mr Niels', and only much later did she discover that his name was Nils. She never says what she thinks of him, but no doubt she was charmed by his ever more frequent visits. He on his part evidently found the Scottish girls attractive. They spoke perfect French, having lived for years in France. They were well-educated in the northern manner, and they could sing. Ann sang duets with Johanna, and also Scottish ballads, accompanying herself on the guitar. She had grave, dark blue eyes, rosy cheeks and luxuriant 'chestnut-blonde' hair.

She enjoyed discussions, too, and held decided opinions. Nils Gustaf really enjoyed her company, and though she might be somewhat serious at times, her younger sister was a chatterbox – a butterfly who gave no more thought than did Carl to 'duties' and other boring matters. But I cannot believe that a pair of blue eyes alone could have detained our roving cavalier if he had preferred other company.

Nils Gustaf was no admirer of Napoleon. He looked with contemptuous distaste upon the Napoleonic dignitaries with whom the family liked to mix, and did not trouble to pick his words when in their elegant drawing-rooms. He regarded the Grand Duke's sluggish administration with a sharply critical eye, and had friends among dangerous characters. Both Mme de Schoultz and Carl were afraid of what their fiery radical might get up to, and warmly encouraged his interest in dear, sensible

Ann, pinning their hopes on her ennobling influence. They were glad when he kept away from people who might start wondering and asking questions; and Mrs Campbell, being so widely-travelled and well-read, was evidently broad-minded enough to take him as he was.

Thus Nils Gustaf made his appearance in Ann's journal and not long afterwards in her mother's red drawing-room.

The journal, which Ann kept with girlish perseverence and discretion, gives a full account of each day's events; yet when describing her walks, tea-parties, musical evenings and visits to churches and galleries in Nils Gustaf's company, she does so coolly – so coolly that one wonders whether her heart ever beat faster when she met M. Nils, or whether she blushed when he gave her flowers. His name, however, is mentioned more and more often.

One evening the whole party went to a concert at the Palazzo Pitti, the Grand Duke's residence, and they arrived so early that they had time to go up to the Boboli Gardens. There they strolled along winding paths under the dark green shade of the cypresses, revelling in the cool of the evening. When they emerged into the golden light of sunset the girls' dresses glowed like jewels. Johanna kept them all amused with the story of her morning call upon 'the queens in exile'. It was cool in the great concert hall, and Ceccherini's solos and choruses were very lovely.

The night was delightful; the evening star on one side of the heavens burned like a little sun, while from Ponte Vecchio we saw the moon rising over the murmuring Arno and casting a pleasant light on the stream. It was very beautiful. Yet our walk home was even more beautiful. We went to tea at Casa Maldura.

This was the home of the Campbells' best friends in Florence: Spence, the famous entomologist, and his charming wife and children. After making polite conversation with Mrs Spence

... we played many funny Swedish games. We laughed awfully and it went unbearably hot. In the middle of the night the thought of the terrace struck us and we asked permission to go up. It was just heavenly. As in duty bound Mlle Johanna and M. Nicolas sung duets to the moon, which was shining beautifully as I said before. After a while as it was rather cold we ran down and found the company taking hot wine.... We had more moonshine as we walked home along the Lungh'Arno with Mlle de Schoultz and her brother.... I fear, my dear journal, thou wilt become noxious with moonshine.

On another occasion Ann and Mary drove out to Mme Catalini's escorted only by M. Nicolas. Again it was raining, but nobody minded, not even when the party was overtaken by a shower in the garden. Everyone dashed up to the house, but Ann preferred to stand under the projecting roof of the orangery and some of the gentlemen promised to rescue her with an umbrella. M. Nicolas stayed with her and they discussed *Orlando Furioso* while water spouted from the gutter pipe.

Next day Nils Gustaf brought Ann a pressed wallflower and begged her to keep it as a memento of their talk in the rain.

More and more often now it was Nils alone who came to Casa Nobili at all hours of the day and night. Johanna had her lessons and singing-practice every morning, and it seems that when Carl was not required to attend her he went elsewhere. The Scots girls learned pretty Swedish songs with incomprehensible words which of course their teacher translated for them. M. Nicolas was a fascinating raconteur and he told incredible stories to his breathless audience; but at times the tales were so unpleasant as to be almost as bad as those of Edinburgh. This one, for instance. Two rich men of Stockholm were to be hanged. One bribed the executioner to let him jump from the cart, and a scarecrow was hanged in his place. The other exchanged his fine clothes for the executioner's rags under the very gallows, and then hanged the man, whose despairing yells were unheeded by the onlookers, and the culprit escaped undetected. That story might have gone down well with the ruffians of the Foreign Legion. Clearly Nils was not quite so polished as he seemed, and Ann did not at all approve of such vulgarity.

Even less did she like the tales of that frightful campaign in Africa and of the sufferings endured by the *légionnaires* in Algeria: the filth, the burning heat and the epidemics which no one could check and which killed off young men by the hundred. When M. Nicolas touched on these subjects, Ann noticed that he used to pale under his sunburn.

It was better when he talked politics. On the question of Poland's struggle for freedom they were at one, with burning conviction. That struggle was admirable, and it was right to side with the Poles against the oppressor. But then M. Nicolas began to censure the Grand Duke's administration, and to express his scorn of the Italians for not throwing such men out of office. How could he have conceived such ideas? Why, they were almost revolutionary! Ann became indignant and angry: one should not meddle in the affairs of others. The Italians were to be pitied, but were they really as contemptible as M. Nicolas made out? They were delightful people, all of them, so there!

M. Nicolas of course made amends. On 8 April Ann wrote in her diary of having

... received a visit from Mr de Schoultz, whose conversation turned I do not know how on the necessary qualifications for his wife, on which subject he got quite échauffé; however he is the only foreigner I ever heard place a man's love for his wife before that for his children, or who seemed to think it necessary that a man should love his wife all the days of his life. ... Mr de Schoultz au contraire is strong upon domestic happiness.

Best of all, M. Nils was conversant with the natural sciences. When the talk turned on them Ann was all enthusiasm. What more natural, then, that M. Nils should offer to instruct her and Mary in physics and chemistry? In return he asked Ann to give him English lessons. Fortunately M. Nils seemed to please Mama. He was ever ready to bring messages from Johanna, and to accompany the girls on their walks to library and post office and scent shop. Mama liked that vaguely cosmopolitan air of his, and found his polished if somewhat brusque manners engaging. He gave the impression of such dependability that she could safely entrust Ann and Mary to his care when she herself had no time to drive out. Mama was having a sad time just now, what with her poor old sister-in-law and certain worrying letters from England, and she may have felt that the young Swede had been sent by providence to her aid. Indeed, one of Ann's granddaughters dared to hint that Mama had been something more than charmed by the serious young man.

In the dark salons of Casa Nobili the Campbell daughters were unaware of any deeper shadows, while in the grand Casa Credi where Johanna sang and Carl danced, all seemed sunshine and delight. Yet there sat Jeanne von Schoultz counting her dwindling ducats. It was expensive to keep two idle young sons lounging about in that gilded society, and Nils Gustaf was giving her real anxiety. He did not even keep suitable company – and yet perhaps – gentle Ann Campbell? Her family was *comme il faut* in every way, and Mrs Campbell was known to be well off. East Indian gold rupees. If only Nils Gustaf could for once see something to his own advantage.

Meanwhile Mary Campbell was reading letters from her bankers in Edinburgh and London. So far, no one but herself knew of the recent financial crashes in India, and for the time being no one need know. There was bound to be enough left for a handsome dowry for Ann. Ann, unluckily, was quite indifferent to marriage plans, and even unaware that a young lady of her age should be considering her future; nor did she seem to read the minds of the young men in attendance on her. But she was always glad to see M. de Schoultz.

Mary Campbell realized that the attentive young Swede had

interrupted his career for some reason, but no doubt in time something might be arranged for him. He was undeniably well-informed and talented. A little nonchalant, perhaps, but he had beautiful manners. He was experienced far beyond his years, and his view of life was based on the noblest principles. The de Schoultz family ranked among the best in their country; she had learnt from the Swedish consul – or was it the minister? – that Mme de Schoultz was the widow of a distinguished man, 'a Swedish count who had been Governor of Finland' [*sic*]. Since his death and the end of the war she had been left in the greatest poverty with five children to educate. For this reason she had come to live abroad and – it was whispered – the pretty daughter with her brilliant musical gifts was to make her début on the concert platform, and perhaps even on the stage of the opera. Yet it was also known that the Swedish royal family were her patrons, and did not regard the de Schoultzes as in any way *declassés*.

What more natural, then, that Mme de Schoultz and Mrs Campbell should be glad for their children to meet?

But there were clear-sighted friends who tried to give warning. A young lady of the English colony had married a German painter, an excellent man; but the affair aroused great indignation. This prompted a woman friend of Ann's to speak to her seriously. Ann was hurt at the mere suspicion, and wrote: 'She may say what she pleases, I think she will hardly find a person more prejudiced against such a thing as I am, but I have never been accustomed to think of it even in the light of a possibility.'

However, Ann did say that she found the German fiancé extremely interesting. She thought his manner towards his bride quite charming; but after the wedding at which she had been bridesmaid she exclaimed: 'It must be very appalling to be married and I wonder where a girl finds courage to make a love marriage!'

Gentle, blue-eyed Ann meant what she wrote. She was also a fairly stubborn young woman.

In the time the young man must have realized what was expected of him. Of course he was in love with the girl; it was inevitable after all the lessons in natural philosophy that he had given her. It is hardly possible to discuss Attraction and Repulsion in the material world without finding parallels on a more rarefied plane. A man can hardly listen unmoved to a soft voice humming Auld Lang Syne, or watch young lips shaping English vowels without longing to kiss them. Everything conspired against the freedom of this lover of freedom. But Ann was very aloof. She even refused to dance the waltz although Mama herself tried to persuade her. On the other hand she was willing to instruct M. Nils in the quadrille and the gallop, which alas proved equally perilous.

What had he to offer her? Where could he take her? It was at this point, so family tradition says, that his strong-willed mother took action. The Scottish ladies were to spend the summer in Siena, in the Contessa Borghese's villa, leaving Florence at the beginning of May. The Contessa's young son Conte Borghese had shown Ann the politest attentions throughout the spring, and who could tell what might have happened by the autumn? Nils must make up his mind now, at once. And so dawned the fateful day.

It was 1 May. Carl and his friend Conte Bandini – or Monsignor Bandini, however one chose to name the stylish and extremely worldly young cleric of Santa Maria Novella – had fetched the girls for a walk, and to invite them to hear music in San Marco next day. M. Nils had private business with Mama. Ann, in a panic, guessed what this might be, and hoped desperately that Mama would give the right answer; Mama knew well enough what her daughter's feelings were. But Mama left the decision to Ann herself – and how should Ann know better than her mother what to say? M. Nils was absolutely nothing

more than 'our favourite acquaintance'. But now Mama explained
to Ann what this proposal might mean for her own future,
and perhaps for that of the whole family. She talked to her
daughter for two hours, and at last Ann promised to think it
over. But she knew what she wanted.

She sat down to think and compose a letter. This was difficult, as she was unwilling to 'hurt his feelings'. The cool May
night wore on and it was four o'clock before the answer was
written. It was a polite, determined No. Dawn broke over the
gables of the Via della Terme.

Next day Nils Gustaf came at the hour of morning tea, which
he drank with Mama and Mary. Ann did not appear: she was
making a fair copy of her letter. M. Charles came to escort
the ladies to the concert and was impatient at having to wait.
At last Ann appeared, and they set off for San Marco.

The great church was crammed. They watched Conte Bandini
officiating at the altar; 'at a distance he looks very handsome.'
The organ music was glorious, but as so often in Catholic
churches there was no reverence: people were walking to and
fro all over the place. The incense was stifling and holy water
was splashed about everywhere. There was constant commotion,
and Ann developed a blinding headache.

The journal tells the rest:

I had the letter with me, so on our way home I gave it to him and
he parted with us at the door. I was sorry then, for I knew it would
grieve him, but I had done for the best, and in the kindest manner
I could. In half an hour he returned, bringing all the books we had
lent him; he was just going off when I met him in the red room,
and as I saw he was on the point of putting his yesterday's promise
into execution of returning to Algiers, I could not have that. In fact
the thing was put before me which I could not pass, though my mind
in the morning was well and not lightly made up, it was impossible
for me now to avoid changing it and had the whole Creation been
there to see I should have done just the same. And so I think would

any woman not utterly hard-hearted and selfish, in my circumstances. If I had disliked him I never could have consented; and in the course of time, and it will require that, I may love him. After I had asked him to wait two years I was frightened, but the thing was done, and as I said before, it was utterly impossible for me to avoid it. I always believed in fate in marriages, but I never knew that it could be so entirely out of your own control.

She continues with touching naïveté:

When Mama came in she was instantly quite reconciled, tho' yesterday she was very unhappy. She said she would walk with him in the Boboli Gardens tonight, and talk *en ami* with him.

She goes on to say – and we can almost hear the sob in her voice:

I never had the idea of such a proposition being in his head, and he even for his own interest has gone a great deal too quickly. It seems to me like a vision ... he was *bien malheureux*. Ah, but if he ever changes I never will forgive myself for my two great softness of heart, and want of firmness – well, enough of this.

7

As it is my Duty...

POOR young people! How could Ann have understood that the man who rushed towards her in the red room was rushing out to Freedom, still shaken by the narrowness of his escape from the snare? Did he realize it himself at that moment? The mothers had won, and they thanked fortune and their own good sense. Mama strolled with Nils in the Boboli Gardens in the cool of that evening, while Ann had to retire to bed after all the excitement.

Such was the end of this sunlit chapter – or was it rather the beginning of something very different?

Nils had indeed begun to spend most of his time at Casa Nobili, and his mother was more than content that he should do so. She had been made increasingly anxious by this unstable, obstinately silent son of hers, who had to be repeatedly explained and introduced to people. Besides, he trailed some very extraordinary friends about with him. Mostly artists. Jeanne suspected many of them of being conspirators of the kind likely to be deported one fine day by the Grand Duke. She had known his eccentric painter-friend Plageman since her years in Sweden, and he at least could be accredited as the painter of Johanna's portrait. He had also won a reputation as a brilliant caricaturist, and his impressions of the beau monde littered the tables of every Florentine drawing-room. Jeanne de Schoultz appreciated such things, but Ann did not. However, Plageman was away from Florence when all this happened, and luckily Nils was to accompany his future family to Siena for a month.

The ladies in the Casa Nobili now had to pack for their summer holiday, and they found the task festive rather than arduous, for Nils Gustaf made himself most useful in seeing to passports, coachmen and last-minute purchases. Sister Mary and he got on very well together: they packed the books while Ann entertained Conte Borghese; she seemed rather too much preoccupied with him when he came to pay his farewell visit, so that Nils was annoyed, and 'this may be wholesome' was Ann's comment.

The parting from Johanna was truly a sad one. Ann gave her a ring, and Johanna wept. Ann and Mary were to pursue their sheltered lives, whereas within a month or two Johanna had to start upon her professional career. Poor Johanna.

The day before departure Nils fell ill, and while everyone was gathering for a festive farewell party at the opera, he was prostrated by one of his severe attacks of fever, and could not come. But Ann, accompanied by Mme de Schoultz, was allowed to visit him and give him a rose. Next day the fever had subsided, but when he came to bid farewell to the travellers he looked so greatly changed, so thin and wretched that it was heart-breaking, 'for it was for our sake that he had exposed himself to the sun and heat'.

The ladies entered the vetturino and bowled away. It was a cloudy morning, but the girls wore white summer dresses edged with pale blue, and new summer hats. Nils's umbrella was left behind in the carriage. They arrived safely at Siena and the Contessa Borghese's villa.

In Florence Nils battled with his fever, in Siena Ann walked about and 'thought': 'I have a good deal to think of, and my meditations tonight were far from happy.'

At last Nils must have got the better of his fever, and he was able to describe a splendid fête, with all Cascine illuminated. He wrote many letters to the Siena address, and Ann mentions them, though without the smallest hint of her reactions. In time, however, she relented enough to confide to her diary that she liked his letters, and that he wrote regularly. Mama often spoke to her about M. Nils and Sweden.

My mother would not change him for any under the sun, foreigner though he be. I who never dreamed of the bare possibility of such a thing have much to combat, and half of my ideas to new-model, and *all* my prejudices to unravel – but as it is my duty, so I doubt not I shall succeed.

How much of his past had Nils confided to Mama? Did she know more of it than was so favourably commented upon by their acquaintances? The glow of romance that surrounded Johanna shed lustre on her impoverished but aristocratic family; and gambling-debts – if any – were nothing to worry about: what more usual than gambling-debts among spoilt young men? Jeanne hardly knew the reason for her son's abrupt departure from Sweden, or anything of his life since then; and it was natural that she should have confided none of her anxieties to Mrs Campbell. Wild youngsters settle down in the end, and Nils had his documents – his officer's commission and the letter autographed by the King – to produce if required. Mama had read them in translation.

May there have been a closer rapport between the twenty-six year old adventurer and the forty-five year old Scotswoman than appeared on the surface? In her youth she seemed to have obeyed the old maxim 'nothing venture, nothing win' when she fled from drab security at home to seek her fortune beyond the seas; and by a bold throw of the dice she had won, when she gave her hand to Alexander Campbell. Now, in the presence of this unknown young man, did she feel something of the same thrill as once she had known with Alexander? With her own brief but radiant married life in mind, she may have fancied that history might repeat itself and allow her to capture a similar happiness for her daughter.

It was Mary Campbell, not Ann, who first succumbed to Nils
Gustaf's charm. This charm was legendary among the Gripenbergs of Voipaala and their descendants. A friend of the grandchildren, speaking of 'the exceptional faculties that have been bestowed on the Voipaala branch of the family' said, 'I am speaking not only of mental gifts. Name a single other family in
Finland which in outward gesture or in sonority of voice, betrays
so true, so aristocratic a nobility as that of the Gripenbergs.
Among even the comparatively less notable members of the
family this characteristic stands out – even Carl Schoultz has but
to lift his hand to reveal this innate nobility of soul.' We cannot
blame Mary Campbell for seeing no further.

Pale, but recovered from his ague, Nils arrived in Siena on
31 May, a day earlier than expected. Ann's little dog received
him rudely, with loud barking. Ann herself was delayed by sheer
agitation; yet although she was gladdened by his coming, no
excitement is discernible in her diary. And henceforth there are
not even any diaries. A note on the cover of volume XXVI
reads: 'Following vols read and destroyed 1861.'

Nevertheless the scenario of that summer in Siena is vividly
described, like a whole series of delicate water-colours linked into
a single panorama. Even the ground-plan of the villa is neatly
drawn in the journal.

The Villa Borghese, which the Campbell ladies rented for the
summer of 1833, was situated outside Porta Carmelia on the road
to Florence. It was built on a steep slope. At first glance it
seemed enclosed, unwelcoming, surrounded by a miserably
neglected garden in a dull and dreary countryside; but when the
girls had sung in the hall and heard its fine acoustics, and had
swept the autumn leaves from the garden paths, they began to
like the place better. Even before M. Nicolas arrived they bought
green hangings to conceal the 'dreadful faces and festoons and
cornucopias with their overflowing fruits which adorned the walls
of the drawing-room!' They shifted the furniture, unpacked their

books, established their household gods [gods: 'Lares et penates'] as it were, and began to feel at home.

Here in Siena, Mary received information which confirmed her fears as to the bankruptcy in Calcutta, and no more payments would be coming from Richards and Mackintosh in London. It was all very alarming, but Ann ends the day's entry with these words:

> I am heartily glad on Mama's account that Nils is coming, it will be a great comfort for her.

Let us hope that this was so; who knows? Nils had out-faced worse threats in his time.

We may safely suppose that the young people did not allow these anxieties to darken their days, and life in the Villa Borghese must have continued much as it began, with reading and reading aloud, letter-writing and a great deal of music. When the heat of the day had passed there were long walks in the cool of the evening. They went into Siena and saw the art treasures in churches and palaces, and no doubt often enjoyed the company of Contessa Borghese and her family as well as that of the charming Grotinellis, who had welcomed the ladies on their arrival with the greatest kindness.

A girl's heart was bound to thaw at last in the warmth of a purposeful adorer. When Nils left at the end of the month, Ann slept with his little blue cap under her pillow.

Then a day or two later, this happened:

> I went to bed last night as usual at half past eleven, put out my candle and was sleeping very quietly, when I do not know how, I came to be thoroughly awaked, and raising myself on my elbow, exclaimed in a tone which I shall never be able to catch again, 'Nils!' for it was he. 'Est ce qu'il est quelque malheur arrivé?' – and yet though hardly believing my senses I was so happy to see him. I do not know how I came to recognize him even before my eyes were open, for he had left the lamp in the ante-chamber, and

the only light my room enjoyed was through the open door. He came and knelt down by my bedside, and on my entreating to know if he was ill – if anything had happened – 'Non, ma chère amie,' he said, 'je suis venu parler à Maman – c'est une chose bien désagréable, mais il faut que je le fasse.'

What was it that had forced the young man to dash headlong back? What was the 'chose bien désagréable' that could not be confided to his future wife? Did Mary Campbell hear the confession which later generations have sought in vain? He must also have written a letter; was it in the hope of being found unworthy of the flowery chains that he had allowed to be hung about his neck? He could have turned to no more tender and understanding a confessor.

'Mon cher fils, comme j'aime de vous appeler par ce titre,' so Mary Campbell begins her reply. She assures him that she has seen enough of the world to be able to discriminate between one character and another, or 'if you prefer to use your favourite expression, j'ai assez de *tacte* pour *sentir* the difference between those who direct their conduct by the deceptive glitter known to the world as honour and glory, and those who take the Word of God in His Gospel as their guideline, and their vigilant conscience as counsellor, and who seek virtue not as an ornament to bombastic speeches, but to convert that virtue into action.' In the same letter Mary assures him that 'almost from the very beginning of our acquaintance I have felt a singular interest, a perfectly unselfish interest' in him, and that she had often reflected how happy must be the mother of such a son.

Let us hope that Mary Campbell received the support and comfort she needed in those anxious days; for it was not only her fortune that seemed to be undermined for all time to come. She was hoping that a merciful death might bring peace to her poor old sister-in-law Christie Campbell, whom Mary had cared for since 1826 when they left Scotland for the continent.

On 5 September she died, aged seventy-seven, and not until then did the ladies return to Florence.

During August, letters had sped between Florence and Siena at least once every three days. Only some of Nils's letters have been preserved, written in French and ending with some Swedish phrase: 'My beloved little wife... my adored girl... Ever your faithful...' The ink is pale, the writing often almost illegible, but one need not spell one's way through many lines before the overwhelming sentimentality of the age reaches one like the scent of dried rose-leaves – a slightly insipid scent – from the yellowed pages. Faithfulness until death, the agonies of longing, praise of the beloved's virtue, her tenderness, purity of soul, trust in God and – excellent upbringing! Once only does the fiancé venture to breathe a hint that on beholding Venus he is aware of more enrapturing treasures – and at once implores forgiveness for this trespass. Yet amid the flood of amorous assurances he strikes a strange note: '... if ever I cease to love you, if ever I desert this Angel may God in heaven strike me down with His wrath for all eternity.'

Before Ann returned to Florence Johanna had left Italy for the dreaded and later fateful stay in Paris. Ann never saw her again. Nils had gone with his family to Leghorn, and not even he could guess that he had taken leave of them for ever.

We know nothing about the winter that followed, except that of the two years' grace promised to Ann she was allowed barely one. On 20 March 1834 the wedding was solemnized in the presence of George Hamilton Seymour Esq, Resident Minister of His Britannic Majesty at the Court of Tuscany, and of Jacob Gråberg of Hemsö, the new Swedish Minister. The ceremony itself is recorded in the register of the English Church in Florence; the day probably followed the pattern customary among the English residents there. Ann had described a friend's wedding the previous spring, and although the half-year of mourning for Aunt Christie had barely elapsed, it seems likely to have been a very festive occasion, with numerous guests. A poem has been preserved, written in Italian and printed on blue paper, with two cornucopias on the cover: *Poemetto Epitalamico/ in occasione/ delle faustissime nozze/ del signore Gustavo De Schoultz con la signora Annetta De Campbell.'* It was composed by Conte Piero Bandini, and dedicated to 'the Noble Lady Maria Alessandra Campbell, best and most enviable of mothers'. Both dedication and poem froth with praise and rapture, in the effusive style of the period and of Tuscany. Perhaps M. Charles had supplied the more impressive particulars of the persons involved, since he himself would shine in their reflected glory.

8

Wedding Journey for Four

THE bridal couple now started on their journey north, but not alone. It would be the bitterest irony to call this a honeymoon. Mary Campbell refused to abandon her daughter to an unknown fate; she went with her, bringing along the headstrong sixteen-year-old Mary. Ann traced the route on thin paper, from Florence via Mantua, Bozen, Innsbruck and Munich to Dresden and Berlin, then Greifswald and finally across the water to Ystad in Sweden. She also recorded exact particulars of the journey: by vetturino in Italy, private coach in Germany, and 'extra post' for the last stretch. The journey took one month and ten days, from 24 March to 2 May 1834, and cost 113 napoleons, 2,260 francs or about £100 for four persons.

The diary which should have described the first stage of the trip is missing. Volume XXXIII, softly marbled in blue and brown, begins at Walchensee in Bavaria. By then they were sitting in Franz Seber's roomy carriage and had become fairly well accustomed to the vicissitudes of travel. There is no alteration in the tone of Ann's journal: it is if possible even more discreet. Hardly does she hint that Nils is there at all; though when she does, it is 'my dear Nils', 'clever Nils' and, as time goes on, a rebellious longing creeps into her account. She laments that she and Nils can never be alone together, and at last she is quite beside herself: 'Oh, newly-married people should *sometimes* be alone, be together away from inquisitive, observant eyes. There is so much to which they must learn to adapt themselves.'

Deep snow lay over the Alps, but already spring was in the air. Sad that they must keep travelling away from it. There is little to be gathered from the conscientiously recorded events of every day, and certainly no hint of romance.

In Munich they suffered an affront: the Duc de Salms smoked at the table d'hôte without even asking permission of the ladies. Nils, however, taught him manners, and an apology was promptly offered. Once Ann's little dog, the beloved Milord, ran away, and Nils 'in his kindness' turned back and found him.

The Bavarian snow was wonderful – if only Nils and Ann could have enjoyed it alone together. But Mary sulked and Mama was cold. Indeed Mama was ill for several days. On the way to Bayreuth they met one of those wretched, wandering soldiers 'en congé'. 'Nils feels such pity for them. He talks to them and always gives them something to help them on their way,' Ann wrote. By the time they reached Dresden a month had passed since their wedding, and 'except for the first day we have never been left alone together!' The young bridegroom's feelings may be imagined.

Nevertheless in Dresden all sorts of pleasant things happened. The very day after their arrival the word had got round that there was a Swedish officer staying at the hotel, and Nils received visits from a grand old Swedish shoemaker and an army man, both of whom were overjoyed at the chance of speaking their native language. And so was Nils. The ladies left cards on a Mme von Düring, who proved a delightful acquaintance. She arranged a little soirée for them and introduced them to many pleasant people. Mama made a real conquest of a Mme von Zitchwitz, who begged her most insistently to return to Dresden one day. The travellers also attended a concert, of which Ann had no great opinion. Here as in Munich they visited churches, museums and royal palaces, and Ann kept a careful record of them all.

On the way to Chemnitz, when there was nothing to look at but dark forests, the company plunged into a lively discussion about the education of women. Nils spoke warmly in favour of serious studies, and of the satisfaction in gaining real proficiency in some particular field. He may have been thinking of Uncle Odert's stimulating ideas. He suggested botany as a subject that ought to interest his little wife, and promised her his help. '... my dear, my good, sweet Nils!'

They reached Berlin and, by an error, the wrong hotel; but they stayed there, despite annoyances of every kind. It was only for three days, for from Baron Löwenhjelm at the Swedish legation Nils found out about sailings from Greifswald to Ystad, and their departure had to be timed accordingly. Nevertheless they put in a great deal of sight-seeing and, best of all, were able to hear Rossini's *Semiramis* at the Italian Opera. *Semiramis* was the opera that Ann had always longed to hear, since all the Italians spoke of it as Rossini's finest work. It was indeed enchanting, and Ann was not disappointed. The brief stay in Berlin was carefree; the next stage of the journey promised to be less so. Roads to the north were said to be abominable, and as for Ystad – the ladies could have no idea!

They started the last lap of their long journey in sunshine. Berlin looked magnificent as it slowly vanished in the morning haze. Ann was always to recall this city with a special tenderness, for it was here that she enjoyed some of her few hours alone with Nils, which gave her more delight than anything else. We can see from this that Nils had won her trust and devotion. She wrote nothing about this in her journal, which was intended as a factual record; yet one detects a new and moving intensity in her descriptions. The pen of the diarist seems to run as an accompaniment to some inward process, which remains her own secret. Yet despite the dawning warmth it sounds like a finale in a minor key – or if not a finale, then the saddest of preludes.

Evening came over the endless plains. The road wound along the shore of a glittering lake, beyond which beech trees spread their tender green like a canopy, above a herd of feeding swine. Soon all this was left behind, and the road ran straight forward into infinity. Nils and Ann alighted from the carriage and took a long, pleasant walk, but they regained their places on approaching a village. Oh, those miserable, ruinous, ugly villages huddled within half-breached walls, empty and desolate, marking the hideous trail of war. Nils knew all about that. But when he had taken Ann on a tour among cabins and pigs and other livestock, and she had enjoyed a really good supper with dark, sweet Mannheim ale served by a pretty girl, she began to think that life was not so terrible after all. If only – she *did* so wish that she was beautiful! But Nils assured her that he loved her just as she was.

Next day had barely dawned when at five o'clock the travellers rose bravely from their beds. They were now faced with an adventurous journey along a road described by everyone as hopeless. At first it was not so bad. In places the crops stood thick and high against the carriage windows, and the air was clear and cool. They saw about thirty ploughs busy in the same field, and behind every pair of horses ran a foal. At Greiffenberg they had to pay toll, and their splendid coachman, whom Ann called Monkey, was full of back-chat, as usual. The countryside had grown marshier and mistier. At the walls of Prenzlau the road ended, and the travellers had a foretaste of what they might expect, for when they

passed a body of troops exercising in a damp and low plain immediately under the fortifications, every creature who saw our heavily loaded carriage turned with surprise to look again, marvelling if we were in our right senses when we were thinking of entering the marsh with so much baggage.

And sure enough, when after a couple of hours' rest they set forth again and rolled out through the gate on the other side of the town, leaving paved streets behind them, they beheld their route in all its horror, with deep, narrow wheel-ruts and more broken up and pot-holed than any road they had ever seen. After only twenty-five yards of it they knew that no description had been exaggerated. They met timber-wagons advancing as slowly as themselves. On either side of the road was a deep ditch lined with willows. As the horses could move at no more than a walk, the passengers alighted and made their way on foot for two hours, yet without daring to go ahead of the carriage, as Nils had continually to lend a hand and prevent it overturning altogether. And so they walked and walked, beneath an overcast sky.

They had a half-hour meeting with a horseman of Swedish descent, dating from the time when Pomerania was a Swedish possession. He led them up on to a hillock to point out the surrounding country and describe the most recent wars. Dusk fell. Rain fell. At last they came to trim little Pasewalk, with its trim, inviting inn. But a rogue there urged them to go further – only one German mile along a decent paved road. They took this bad advice.

The sun had set and they bowled along at a good pace through the gathering darkness. Soon they could

distinguish only the boundary of the vast fields mingling with the pale line of the sky; and then at either side we distinguished the red and perfidious lights of the Ignis Fatuus, glancing for a moment, and disappearing. I do not know what impression this deceitful glimmer produced upon me, in this wild and solitary place. We are in safety, but how many it may have lured on to destruction, and when we give a loose to our imagination, it seems as if the Spirit of Evil had power and leave at such an hour to work out the ruin of those who are alone and friendless under the vast vault of night. Ah, if there were not a God in heaven, what should we do . . .

When at last they arrived at Gastruck, no inn whatever was to be found! The miserable little hamlet had never had pretensions to such a thing. They had to seek lodging for the night in a dirty peasant cabin full of smoking men. There was no bed, and Ann would rather have stayed in the carriage; but Mama would have no squeamishness, so the party settled down as best they might on benches and straw, while Ann's little dog Milord lay on a sack of chaff in the corner.

All the same, it was not such a bad night, and next morning at sunrise they left the place to continue their anxious and lamentable journey. They were guided on to a road which, like Penelope's web, seemed never likely to end; and along this they struggled between miry ruts, through that endless marshy country. Ann invoked death and destruction upon the King of Prussia.

The morning was beautiful beyond all description, and while Mama and Mary slept in the carriage, Ann and Nils jumped quietly out and walked on slowly under the arch of glorious beeches that were strewn with the first green of spring. Young leaves lay lightly as snowflakes upon the branches, transformed by the new season. Squirrels dashed up and down the tree-trunks, making merry with the last of their stored nuts, and in their rust-red coats scrabbled through the withered leaves upon the ground.

... How happy one could live midst scenes as fair and free as this, midst summer leaves and under a summer sky.

I cannot help wishing sometimes Nils and I had liberty to breathe the air of nature in solitude together, but it seems that will never be – and however the after months may be, the first months of the marriage of two young people are better spent alone together. We are not of the same nation, and have much to learn, perhaps even of each other.

When Ann tired, she climbed up on the box again. The road became ever sandier, and was crossed continually by other tracks. At some such point they must have gone astray, for when at last they arrived at a small hamlet they found that they had come some distance along the road to Mecklenburg. The weary horses had to turn back and, now with a guide, the party continued their journey along sandy forest paths until they emerged once more into a desert landscape of sand, more sand, and enormous boulders. Here and there among the rocks were clusters of dismal trees, then marshes and meres. Nils rescued a brood of goslings and fetched them up on to dry land through a fence to their stupid mother, who had carelessly abandoned them.

Without further adventures the party arrived at a dilapidated inn in Ferdinandshof. While the landlady was fussing over the coffee the travellers held council over what was next to be done; for now the hitherto dauntless Monkey declared that the horses could go no further. At this opportune moment the post-master appeared; he knew the true state of the roads. From that point onwards these roads were if possible even worse, and the only solution was to take an 'extra post' – the local term for a conveyance that, unlike the ordinary diligence, could be hired at any time of day – and for the baggage a cart having the right width between the wheels for the roads hereabouts. The post-master offered them his own carriage and four, and a cart and pair for the baggage.

Coachman Monkey was not a little proud of the sensation he aroused among the villagers, who soon gathered about him and his *equipage* to hear of his adventures along the road. When at last everything had been settled up, and Nils had written Monkey's testimonial in both German and English, he gaily took his leave, kissing Mama's hand and turning his horses' heads back towards his cheap, snug lodging in Gastrup.

The travellers bade the good post-master farewell and set off in a roomy, light berline and four, trotting briskly through mud and mire to a rousing horn trio from the three postillions. At about four o'clock they drove in through the gates of the little fortified city of Anklam. Here the inn was beautifully clean and neat, with brass locks on the doors, as in Scotland. They dined well and, while it was still daylight, slipped into their inviting beds, saving the tallow candles for when they rose at two in the morning to resume their journey to Greifswald. They had heard that the boat for Ystad would sail at eleven.

It was the first of May. Little had Ann dreamt a year ago that destiny was to carry them all to far-away Sweden.

They got up by starlight, with a posthorn sounding before the steps, and entered the carriage in darkness. It had been raining and it was cold, but they did their best to fall asleep again. In the grey light of dawn they saw wet horses standing in motionless slumber in the endless fields. The flat landscape, varied by strips of woodland here and there, began to show that they were approaching the sea. It became bitterly cold, and poisonous vapours seemed to rise from the marshes. 'At last the line of ocean caught our eyes. I have not seen it since we left Pisa – and here it joys me not. Is it strange that there I should look upon it as the eternal barrier betwixt me and my native land?'

By nine they were in Greifswald, and at the sight of its deserted little streets the travellers felt gloomy forebodings of what Ystad would have to offer. It would be just as every travelling Swede had told them! Nils hurried to the Swedish consulate to change the last of their money. After paying thirty-seven francs for the crossing they had eight louis d'or left; but Nils returned with a letter of credit for an unlimited sum on a Mr Gran in Ystad. Nils was as happy as a child to think that no money-worries awaited them in his country; and so were they all. 'Pray God our present reasonable expectations may be fulfilled.'

Ann found a letter waiting for her from Eleonor Gråberg. They entered the carriage again and drove down to the harbour.

What a small boat! Fifty-two horse-power, and paddle-wheels twelve foot in diameter. They had a long wait for the post, but punctually at three o'clock it arrived, manned by two smart seamen in blue uniforms and with shiny brass badges in their hats. The Prussian black double eagle was hoisted and slowly they glided away from land. They were bound across the sea, but '. . . not going home! No doubt it is sad to Mary – perhaps it is to Mama – but oh, they have not forgone their native land as I have done. These blue waters which might bear me to my native land are taking me from it – is it forever?'

They all tried to be cheerful. But in the night stillness, as the paddles churned their monotonous cascades, the young couple paced the deck, their tears falling fast.

Both had a premonition of difficult years to come. Ann dreaded the unknown future; Nils had to meet a past from which he had once fled, and of which the shadow never paled. All trace of it seems to have vanished, and only hints touch upon unspoken things. Many years later Ann, in the introduction to her English translation of Fryxell's history, wrote:

. . . and should this translation ever fall into the hands of the generous Crown Prince of Sweden – now King Oscar I – may it bear to him the grateful thanks of a heart that has long sought to acknowledge her obligation to one who, when one word would have crushed, forebore to pronounce that word.

Hardly had the new arrivals settled in Ystad when their troubles began. A disputed bill of exchange was the first welcome they received. Mary Campbell sent a cry for help to London – and it was not to be the last. Her sister Elisabeth Phillips was appalled:

I am so unhappy and filled with dread lest you should find yourself in such a painful embarrassment that I do not know what to think. A thousand most painful ideas will present themselves which I try to banish! I wish you would write and say what has caused this protest – is it a bill for *military pay refused?* or how should it be without his knowledge – so unexpectedly – has he not friends! *no one* in his own country who could prevent such a *small* sum throwing you into such confusion and that at such a time too! Can his father's son get no help at his Court? or is there no one known to him who would prevent him applying to his wife's friends for such a trifle? Write for Heaven's sake and explain this for it is impossible to think otherwise than anxiously ... what can still happen ... I am really alarmed ... I can wait no longer. I shall send the money at once.

Nils had to eat humble pie. He hastened to Gothenburg where he hoped to find his father's sister and her husband – his dear foster-parents, as he called them – but Colonel de Frese and his lady had left the town. However Nils met his younger brother Edvard, now studying at Chalmers, and borrowed money from him; then having obtained Aunt Ulrique de Frese's address in Karlskrona he hurried back to the ladies in Ystad. From there he wrote a letter which has been piously preserved, and which later generations have tried in vain to interpret:

Heavily has the hand of the Almighty lain upon my head, yet I bless him who through the profound sufferings of body and mind that he sent me, restored me to my senses and taught me that it is in religion alone that man finds his true bliss. Little did you, my inexpressibly dear Aunt and my respected foster-father imagine in 1831, as you lay down to rest at night, that the unhappy Nils who for so long enjoyed with you all the rights of a son, was wandering barefoot through France, half-naked, half-starved and half dead from cold; and later that, as a private soldier, he made the campaign in Africa against those savages who show no humanity to their stricken foes. Many a time did I reflect with envy upon my dog, whom I had left in the care of my brother Fredrik. He had a far better life than I. I now enjoy the ineffable peace inspired by the knowledge of my reconciliation with God. I dare to believe that he has forgiven me the extravagances of my youth, and it now remains for me to atone for faults in two other respects, namely towards my nearest and dearest, and towards the affronted land of my birth ... and it may be that at the hour of death I shall be surrounded by those whose blessings will accompany me beyond the grave, and intercede for me before the throne of the Almighty.

Across this letter he wrote: 'I beg you not to mention my arrival yet; I have good reason to remain unknown for the present. This is most necessary, until I shall receive further letters from Landgren, the Judge of Appeal in Stockholm.'

Among the files of the Svea Court of Appeal no letter or other document is to be found relating to Lieutenant von Schoultz.

He further implores his foster-parents to forgive all his aberrations, and declares that through hard trials he has been brought to a better frame of mind, and can perceive the Almighty's forgiveness in the happiness that has now been bestowed upon him in his young, innocent and noble-minded wife.

The affectionate foster-parents forgave him, and made haste to rent house and furniture for him, to hire servants and arrange credit, and they welcomed Nils and his interesting foreign family in the most cordial way. Tradition has it that everything Mary Campbell brought with her in the way of silver and linen had to be sacrificed to pay her son-in-law's debts. Debts to whom?

Poor Ann, her worst fears were exceeded by reality, and life must have seemed overwhelming. The splendid castles that Nils had shown her in the Swedish minister Gråberg's engravings and had described so vividly, were now infinitely remote, hidden within their windswept parks. The amiable, aristocratic young people of whom Carl had spoken never drove up to the door; they were not even aware that a young Fru von Schoultz existed, and was awaiting callers.

9

Edinburgh: City of Dreams

OF the first winter in Karlskrona no diaries have been preserved. Whether any part of Nils Gustaf's past had been revealed to his wife I cannot tell, but from letters to relations in England it is clear that Mary Campbell was not easily daunted. She contrived to straighten out some of the muddles, and remained the prop and stay of the little family. Ann too did her best. Her duty now was to learn to be a Swedish housewife, with all that this implied of 'ridiculous duties'. She also continued to keep an accurate record of the day's doings; this she regarded as an obligation. It was a sort of balance-sheet to be submitted to the Lord, as well as a lesson to be studied, reflected upon and learnt from. But this diary was not left for the eyes of posterity: 'read and destroyed 1861.'

We find no hint that a baby was expected, and no record of its birth on 9 January. 'A perfectly beautiful little daughter,' as Nils later wrote to his maternal uncle Sebastian in Finland. She was christened Mary Henriette. Long afterwards Ann added the name of Florence by which she was always called and which has descended to the girls of the fourth generation. But in her father's letters she was referred to as Little Tuttan, as also in her mother's diary, where she is mentioned for the first time in late summer. But 'diary' is hardly the name for the pitiful fragments left for later eyes, from which everything that we would most like to know has been excised. The gaps are the more moving. The pages are collected together and enclosed within the soft yellow binding of Giorgio Vasari's *Le vite dei più eccellenti pittori* . . . printed in Florence, 1834. Ann seems to be saying that everything she afterwards experienced must be seen in the light of those wonderful years in her beloved Tuscany. There are many odd scraps of different kinds of paper, written on with different inks, sometimes dated, more often not. Nevertheless these fragments do link up to form pictures in which Nils appears, whether actively or as a self-evident figure in the background.

A coherent account begins on 26 September 1835 – not July, as was later written in above. At that time the young couple appear in Edinburgh, preparing to start for home. When or how they arrived there, or why, was discovered in a little packet of closely-written letters that unexpectedly appeared from out of the past.

The purpose of the journey was clear. Nils was to be presented to the family, and Ann could see her beloved country again. Most important of all, Mary Campbell's belongings were to be fetched from Scotland to her new home in Karlskrona, and her confused money affairs straightened out if possible. They may have written to Elisabeth Phillips in London, and made inquiries about their passage, yet it seems as if the decision and departure were sudden and quite unexpected. Evidently Elisabeth Phillips had written to say that she and her two daughters were on the point of leaving for Scotland, and the idea that Ann and Nils might meet them there no doubt clinched the matter.

Nils, a master at quick decisions, seized the first opportunity to sail; and thus it was that early in the morning of 4 August 1835 he and Ann found themselves aboard Captain Pålson's newly-built little vessel *Naiad* when, towed by the frigate *Carl Johan*, she glided slowly out of Karlskrona. Once out in the roads she was left to catch the wind in her own sails, and stood away towards open water. However hasty the departure, pen, ink and paper had not been forgotten, and it was not long before

Ann began her first letter to her dear mother, to be taken ashore by the pilot when he left the *Naiad*.

She sat on a little barrel in the bows to write, enjoying the warm, lazy morning breeze. The little waves in the wide bay glittered, and the August sun was almost too hot, but thoughtful Captain Pålson had a sail rigged as an awning for the young lady. Nils, with the captain's help, was arranging her cabin below. Ann's dream voyage had begun.

Slowly, lingeringly the vessel moved out, further and further from the town, yet still near enough for Ann to hear the clock in the tower strike nine, and the roll of drums in the market-place. She would certainly have seen Mama and Mary if they had come out of their door, for their street, Vallgatan, with its friendly little houses, remained in sight to prolong the pain of parting. '... Oh, how many times I shall think of you, my dear Mother,' Ann began, 'and how much I already long to be back. May God keep you and my innocent child.... I am sure God will permit me to find you all well on our return. Oh, my little angel, my heart is weeping.' But she adds at once in resignation, '... and believe me that this unlooked for voyage shall turn out for all our pleasure, profit and advantage.'

We also learn that Mary Campbell had provided them generously with food for the journey, that the cook Maria's fresh bread tasted fine and that Aunt de Frese's ham was delicious. They had had an excellent breakfast and Nils had been very hungry.

Ann also reminds her dearest Mother to write at once to Aunt Elisabeth and tell her that Ann and Nils are on their way, and that she is on no account to leave Scotland before they get there. It would be wonderful if this voyage were as fortunate as Captain Pålson's last one, when he sped in the *Naiad* from Hull to Karlskrona in nine days. So, if Aunty could only wait, if luck was with them, and the wind and weather, etc. etc.

Unhappily it was not to be. Next day the first gale swept

over them like a hurricane. They had to seek shelter in Karls-
hamn, and from here Nils sent the first letter he ever wrote
to his mother-in-law in English. Earlier ones are all in French.

Carlshamn
9 August 1835

Dearest Mother! I see your astonishment in receiving our letters
dated from this place, but the stormy weather forced us to enter here
and I am most thankful to God that we could enter too. Our little
vessel is certainly a good one, that is true, but the sea was so high
and the storm so strong that we after 3 days constant labouring were
very glad to get a pilot to conduct us in this beautiful and romantic
port and I cannot express my joy to see my dear little Anna so glad
and free on board this ship; she has gained everyone's heart and
from the Captain to the cook they delight in paying her every attention in their power. Also I am sure that the Captain had not yet
entered the port (because it costs him 30 riksdaler) had it not been
for [her]. He is really an excellent and good man, and insists
that not one Swedish Lady can be compared to my Anna for courage
in a storm, and that the sailors look with glad surprise and wonder
towards her. I wished you had been with us to enjoy the view we
had in the storm, above all the third day when our little ship was
boarded by waves three times higher than the vessel itself, but run
and cut through them and jumped over them as easy as your
Job's wild ass should have gone through a flock of large stupid
cows.

Dear Anna, she troubles herself on your account and I am really
not calm myself when I remember that you are left in a country
whose language is unknown to you. But God in his mercy will
preserve you to us all. You must not worry about my misfortune [?].
Greet Maria, Carolina and Nora. I hope they are behaving well as
they promised and make no trouble to you.

The little *Naiad* was soon able to resume her voyage, but it
was no dream-trip. She had to cruise up and down Hanö bay
for a long time before coming out into the Sound. There she
rocked, becalmed, on the shining swell amid countless craft

from east and west which like her were all waiting for the wind. Nils and Ann read the name *L'Imperatore* on one graceful vessel as she glided by, and when Nils called out 'Siete italiani?' the reply came promptly in an operatic tenor: 'Si-siii!' Delightful word! The couple played écarté and patience. Ann got through *Orlando* – she did now know how many times she had read it before – and while she hesitated between heroic Tasso and divine Dante for her next reading, another storm burst over them. The days went by. It was wet and cold and miserable, and the ninth day was long past when they were still nearer the Norwegian coast than that of Scotland. On the 22nd they were off the Dogger Bank and Ann was in despair. 'We shall arrive too late.'

The thirty-eight closely-written pages tell just what it was like in the year 1835 to travel from Karlskrona to Hull in a sailing ship manned by the skipper and a crew of four. Despite all adversity those on board were in good spirits. The seamen were splendid, and so was Captain Pålson, Ann wrote; and they in their turn praised her cheerfulness. A real friendship grew up between them during those frustrating weeks. When the passengers' food supply gave out, they started on the skipper's sack of ship's biscuit. Pålson took the tenderest and most fatherly care of 'the Gracious Lady', and she speaks of her regard for him in her letters. Of Nils she has little to say; her letters are filled for the most part with sighs of longing for her mother and little daughter. If ever she had yearned to be alone with Nils and to travel far out in the world with him, she now had her wish. But it came too late.

The timid tenderness for Nils which seemed to be springing up in her heart during their arduous journey north must have been permanently frost-nipped by the calamities that befell them on arrival in her new country. Nils had never concealed his poverty from her, or denied that privations awaited them, but the disputed bill of exchange at Ystad he had not foreseen

and could not have avoided. The extremity that had forced the
proud Scots to send that cry for help to the family in England
came as a crushing blow. It was Mary Campbell who took the
brunt of it, and she who must have helped her daughter through
pregnancy and childbirth. Is it any wonder that she remained the
one firm support in Ann's life?

Mary Campbell may have been right in suspecting a longing
for affection and domestic happiness in the broken young man
who was presented to her in Mme Catalani's salon, but she
ought soon to have recognized his unfitness to care for a childish
and hopelessly spoilt wife. Who knows whether he had the
patience to love anyone who was neither brilliant nor beautiful,
nor willing to revise certain firmly-implanted notions of conscientious behaviour. Everything suggests, too, that poor little
Ann had no idea how to deal with him. In today's worn-out
terms we should say that Nils was too immature for responsibility and incapable of a warm and lasting affection, while Ann
had an incurable mother-fixation.

Such is the lamentable story to be read between the lines of
letters from the luckless little vessel, which sailed from Karlskrona in serene summer weather and dropped anchor in Hull,
in rain and fog, twenty-two days later.

Nothing could be seen of Hull except that it was flat and
black under billowing smoke. Rain was falling in torrents, and
Ann never even attempted to go ashore – 'I should have
drowned!' – but Nils and Captain Pålson set off at once to buy
food and fetch mail. They returned gleefully with letters from
Karlskrona, and some fine sole, which they ate as their spirits
rose.

Dear Mother, you should have seen Nils on his return from this
excursion, with what sparkling eyes he recounted his first expedition
in England. How that they had gone into the meat market to buy
fish, and that an Hotel where they wanted 'sole' a lad brought them
slippers thinking they should sleep there, and finally conversation

with the fishwoman in the fish shop, when he said, 'Oh my dear Mistress, you are too dear, I shall never come to you again.'

One wonders what Mama made of this ingenuous letter.

The *Naiad* docked next day and at last, on 27 August, Ann once more set foot on English soil.

Everything was very different from what she had expected. People rushed about madly, yelling in hoarse voices. Nils said that the women and girls, of whom there seemed to be strangely many in the streets, clumped along taking huge strides with big feet, as if testing the strength of the paving-stones. Customs formalities took so long that they missed the morning diligence to Edinburgh. Instead they caught the one to York, at eleven, and from there drove post to Scotland.

They reached Edinburgh in sunshine. Leaving their luggage at the hotel – Mrs Moffat's, 28 James Square, where with hands that trembled Ann changed her clothes – they drove out to Blackford House, the paradise of Ann's childhood. Would they find Aunt Elisabeth there, or at least one of the girls? Ann cherished a faint but persistent hope that dear, sensible Miss Trotter, their old friend, would have induced them to delay their departure. Yes, and Miss Trotter's happy 'Welcome, welcome!' would help them to survive even if . . .

It was some time before the door opened.

Mrs Phillips and the young ladies had left a fortnight before. Miss Trotter had gone on a long visit to a friend in Musselburgh. The strange parlourmaid did not invite them in, and they stood on the doorstep for a moment that seemed an eternity. Nils found time to appreciate the warm, summery, silent dignity of the old house, and caught a glimpse of roses beyond the neatly-clipped box hedge. He saw the tops of tall trees against the blue of the sky. Then they walked back to the carriage.

Nils had to wipe away Ann's tears as they drove back into Edinburgh. They decided to pay another call at once and get it over: a necessary one, which they looked forward to with mixed feelings. John Archibald Campbell, Ann's cousin, who had looked after Mary's affairs in Edinburgh, had now to be consulted about business matters and the packing up of Mary's possessions. He was the son of Ann's eldest paternal uncle, and certainly older than this Aunt Mary of his, who was always getting into some scrape or other. It is clear that Mary Campbell had little fondness for him, while he on his part had every reason to be concerned about her many unexpected enterprises and might not be pleased at the sudden appearance of his young relatives in Edinburgh.

John Archibald was away.

The whole family had gone to England, and the house was full of joiners and painters. However, John Archibald was expected home in two days' time. This was more than a disappointment; it was a near-disaster, in view of the von Schoultzes' meagre funds.

Mrs John Campbell and her daughters, Ann's dearest cousins from the time of her childhood in Scotland, had moved with bag and baggage to settle for good in Cheltenham.

Ann was stunned. But what could they do? Leaving a letter for John Archibald they made their arrival known to Miss Trotter, who at once invited them out to Musselburgh.

There all was as Ann had hoped. Miss Trotter was not only as kind and delightful as ever, but was really charmed by Nils and inquired with interest after the baby, after Mama and little Mary, who she supposed was now a young lady. On their return they found John Archibald's visiting card at the hotel, and things began to move.

Nils wrote a day or so later:

Now, my dear Mother, you will be astonished to hear what I have to say of J. A., but certainly he has conducted himself towards us as a brother – he has spared no trouble to serve us. You must know, dear Mother, that he has taken a great fancy for me and I for him. He appears to like Ann as his sister, and that does my heart so good. . . . Well then, when we met first he showed us his house, which was under reparation unfortunately, so that there was no possibility of our having your trunks and other things down from the garret because from the bottom of the house to the top a scaffold was raised by the painter and plasterer, and this scaffold will not be down before some days . . .

There was more packing to be done, however, at the house of the Misses Fullerton, in India Street, and there too the young people were received with the greatest kindness. The 'three old ladies, the eldest about forty-five years', offered them breakfast the first morning. The house belonged to Mary Campbell, and Nils was able to report that it was in perfect condition, being maintained by John Archibald.

Business affairs as well were settled in the pleasantest manner. Mary had at last managed to have money sent from India to Baring Brothers in London. Ann writes fully, clearly and tactfully to her mother about all these arrangements. First, longstanding loans from John Archibald and Thomas Phillips must be repaid. The former firmly refused to accept more than £500 and, if Mama was determined to give more than £300 to Uncle Thomas, John Archibald would reduce his share still further; for Nils had hit on a admirable idea. Mama was to lend out £400 in Sweden where she could get 6½ per cent, which was considerably more than was obtainable here. Nils himself was willing to borrow this sum from her, offering as security the life insurance he had just taken out for Ann – with money that was due to her. How this transaction developed is not known, as no reply to the proposition has ever been found. Nils needed the money to start farming, and as the various sums amounted to rather more than Mama had authorized them to collect in London, John Archibald was willing to help, for he had taken an exceptional liking to the young man. Ann repeats his comments:

He is an *above-board* man. He goes to business straight at once. I consider him as a gentleman, not only by his manners for that is a small matter, many a *scoundrel* may have good manners, but by his thoughts. If I had not, I tell you frankly, I would not have taken him to Lady Strathmore.

For John Archibald introduced Nils to this relative of his at church on Sunday. Lady Strathmore held a high position at Holyrood House, so Nils was able to visit that famous palace.

Good John Archibald showed his favour in an if possible even more convincing way. After entertaining his young cousins at Sunday dinner, he sent for soda water and glasses, and brought out a bottle of whisky, feeling that Nils, after all his laborious and dusty packing, deserved a glass of 'our national drink'. This whisky was unique, and was no longer made. It was twenty-five years old, and once the bottle was empty John Archibald would never again enjoy the flavour of this marvellous liquor which he now offered to Nils. Nils appreciated the honour. What he thought of the taste Ann does not say.

Surprisingly enough there was time for sight-seeing, for the expected letter from Captain Pålson about their sailing-date had not arrived. Ann was more than ready to return home. Her longing for her child was growing ever harder to bear. Mrs Moffat's bill was lengthening in an alarming manner, while Nils and Ann had nothing much to do in the town, which everyone had left for the summer. Nils of course had seen all there was to see of things old and new, and was enthusiastic and impressed.

As there was still no news of Captain Pålson, Nils went to Glasgow to inspect the new factory buildings of Messrs Monteith and Hamilton, mainly no doubt to show them a red dye that he had manufactured, of which he hoped great things. Two letters survive, from Nils to Ann, written in Glasgow. He describes what he has seen there, but seizes the opportunity to ask her for money. More of this was always needed than had been allowed for, and Mary Campbell had evidently felt it safest to entrust the journey-money to her daughter, which was embarrassing to all three.

But Nils was delighted with his expedition. He had also visited the famous botanical Gardens of Glasgow and had been presented with 'an unusual plant, said to produce an exceedingly beautiful blue dye'. Of the industries he had seen he wrote with keen admiration:

Indeed, my dear Anna, it is delightful to see your English [sic] great establishments. How immense the scale is upon which every one of these are constructed, and when you hear that Mr Monteith's is one of the largest you can imagine how wast [sic] it is. Seven miles out of Glasgow he has a whole village with about 2,000 souls where his cotton is spun and twined.

All this was most stimulating to a man of imagination. Natural sciences, engineering and chemistry seemed to hold the keys of mankind's future paradise, and if Nils was conversant with anything it was with these very subjects, in addition to mathematics. He had maintained his interest in them since his schooldays with Uncle Odert Gripenberg, and as far as possible kept abreast of new developments. Now he began to dream of personal success in these fields, as well as in agriculture.

No letter came from Captain Pålson, and Ann had time to add to her journal, which she would bring to an end and post before going aboard the *Naiad*. The last page is chiefly a record of Nils' successes. He had every reason to feel pleased, she wrote, fêted as he had been everywhere. Sir John Sinclair had invited him and John Archibald Campbell to luncheon, and given him his *Code of Agriculture*. John Archibald gave him three volumes of the *Transactions of the Highland Society*. From Aunt Archy he received a wooden snuff-box which had something to do with Mary, Queen of Scots. Mr Hamilton of Glasgow fancied that a live arrowroot plant in a pot could be sent to Sweden, to furnish material for fresh experiments. Mr Oswald, one of the masters at Heriot's Hospital, presented him with a summary of his method of teaching English. Wherever Nils went, he found favour, 'as usual'.

Ann sounded happy when she wrote this: 'My poor Nils, who has been so badly treated and so badly considered. But God was with him and will yet lift him up ... the luck has changed, perhaps, and God has not forsaken us.'

Still no sign of life from Captain Pålson. He had begged them most urgently to hurry with their packing. At last Nils went down to Newcastle where they had agreed to meet, and found him waiting there, really disturbed about his missing passengers. It was later discovered that his letters had been delivered at Schultz the tailor's in Newhaven! Nils hurried back, and next day he and Ann left Edinburgh.

This last day was appropriately rainy and dismal. John Archibald had rejoined his family in England, and Nils had only cards p.p.c. to leave on Lady Strathmore at Holyrood House and Sir John Sinclair at the Castle. Ann did not go on this hasty tour, though she drank one last glass of ginger ale with Nils at Aunt Archy's: the aunt who makes an unexplained appearance in the journal, and who must have been the widow of one of Ann's six uncles. On the way back to the hotel they bought a fine pair of gloves for Nils and *Blackwood's Magazine* for Ann. At the very last minute when they called at Law's for a pound of Mocha coffee, Nils made Ann go in and inspect the ingenious coffee-roasting machines.

Mrs Moffat's bill was paid and, accompanied by Aunt Archy, they drove for the last time through the streets of Edinburgh – the town that had received them with closed doors, and where Ann had felt abandoned by everyone. Yet she left the city of her childhood with a sad heart. The road to Newhaven, so well-known to her of old, was unchanged. Trees, buildings, everything was as it had been in former days – but of, the difference!

... and yet, what know I of change but in myself, but I can never be the same again. Where is the Ann Campbell of yore? gone, changed, though not dead, and yet, how fair this land is!

Ann was inconsolable, but Nils seemed eager to be on his way once more. On his way! That was the breath of life to him. One last shower of rain swept over them as they walked out along the stone jetty to their boat. The day was ending, and no evening could have been drearier for a leave-taking. Darkness had fallen before they could make sail, and what with rainclouds and evening mist little could be seen. But the hills, the hills were there, enclosing the kingdom of Fife and the Firth of Forth in their graceful curves, rising height beyond purple height against a threatening sky. They vanished now and sank into the west. Nils cared nothing for all this, and why should he? Ann sat up on deck as long as she could see anything at all, watching the vanishing city and mighty, now barely discernible silhouette of its Guardian Lion, and the cone of light that kept its constant watch. 'Oh, I shall not soon see it,' she mourned.

They were to make first for Newcastle, where they hoped to find Captain Pålson. Then all their luggage had to be transferred to the *Naiad* which lay laden at her berth in Sunderland, where the final customs formalities had to be completed. A steady, favourable wind beneath a starlit sky brought them early to the mouth of the Tyne.

Newcastle, with its canopy of thick smoke, was visible from a long way off. Apart from this, the sea-approach was beautiful, with the winding river, the hills and city spires in the background, the bridges, and the forest of masts. At last they tied up at their berth below a big warehouse, amid a swarm of other vessels. Passengers and baggage were taken ashore, and hardly had Ann changed and sat down to breakfast at the Turf Hotel when Captain Pålson appeared, delighted at having come upon his belated passengers so quickly. He had waited a fortnight for them – two weeks of favourable wind! They must now sail as soon as possible before the weather changed, as it threatened to do.

Pålson and Nils got busy at once with customs and trans-shipment to Sunderland. The skipper wanted to leave next morning, so although it was Sunday the two men succeeded in completing all their preparations. Early on Monday morning they sailed down-river, but now in a small paddle-steamer. Visibility was good. The weather was very cold, and bearable only when one kept close up against the boiler; there was also a constant shower from the paddles. But there was life and activity all round them.

Countless chimneys along the shore sent up their billowing smoke. For every tall one, a score of others could be counted among the factory furnaces and brick works. In places, where the shoreline was low, the railway came right down to the water; here coal was loaded into ships that would carry it all over the world. Their own vessel took cargo on board on her way out, so Nils and Ann could see how it was done.

South of the Tyne the coast is open to the North Sea, and there followed a rolling, drenching passage in the little paddle-steamer; Ann was thankful when she saw ships lying at anchor, and knew that they were now nearing the mouth of the Wear and Sunderland itself which, like all English towns, was crowned by a mighty cloud of smoke. Having rounded the jetty they were safe, despite ebb-tide and breaking seas. Almost at once they found the *Naiad* lying at the quayside, so they could go straight aboard her. There was rejoicing on both sides; merely to step from one deck to the other was like coming home.

Captain Pålson walked off at once with Nils, for there was not a moment to lose. The customs formalities were exasperatingly long-drawn-out, but meanwhile a young man appeared, bringing letters to Ann from Karlskrona. To her great joy, all the news was good.

Nils invited both Captain Pålson and the kindly Captain Emerson, who had so efficiently organized all the preparations here in Sunderland, to a last dinner ashore; it was a feast beyond compare, featuring some stuffed roast mutton which Ann would never forget. Then suddenly, since all their business had been completed so smoothly, Pålson decided to sail that very night.

He and Nils dashed off on heaven knows what final errands while Emerson took Ann to see the famous Iron Bridge over the River Wear. There she could admire the peerless construction of the single, mighty span that swept in a superb arch across the water, and note how incredibly tiny a tugboat looked as, melting into dusk and distance, it towed its little lighter under the bridge. Along the railings on each side ran the device: *Nil Desperandum auspice Deo*. And a fitting motto it was for our impatient travellers, for when they stood on the quay, ready to put out to the *Naiad*, an urgent message arrived for Captain Pålson: the *Naiad* had been rammed by a brig laden with stone! The skipper refused to believe that there had been serious damage, but all the same he was beside himself with anxiety, and swept his party off to the pilot-boat.

The horror of climbing down that slippery, swinging ladder from the quay! Ann could only shut her eyes, while Captain Emerson lifted her down as if she were a doll, to avoid a mishap.

It was pitch-dark when the pilot-boat reached the *Naiad*, but no sooner had Pålson seen her than he ordered everyone ashore again. The *Naiad* had to be unloaded and reloaded. As they were standing there chilled and depressed, surveying the damage, there loomed at them through the mist and darkness a large brig under full sail; but she passed them safely by.

Down into the pilot-boat again, and back to the town.

When at last Ann found herself in Captain Emerson's house she was shivering with fright and cold, but the good man knew how to comfort young ladies in such a plight. She was shown a tiny newcomer who had been welcomed to the home only a day or so before, and its pretty young mother. Then followed a copious tea and a large glass of sherry to end with. 'Now, good luck to you, and a fine little sailor, Mrs von Schoultz!' He guessed at a coming event.

The next time Ann sat down to write up her journal it was Sunday again, 4 October. The *Naiad* lay in calm water under the Norwegian coast, after days of gales and seasickness. 'Spared yet for a while in this world of toil and tears,' Ann wrote, and picked up her account where she had left off. They had sailed at dawn after that calamitous night, with a favourable wind which later changed and drove them almost to Bergen. When the seas broke over the ship Ann's cabin became a shower-bath. Captain Pålson had been unceasing in his care for her, and now all was dry and comfortable again. The *Naiad* lay becalmed under a formidable coastline. Mountains soared to the sky, their summits wreathed in a blue haze that was lit now and again by gliding sunshine. Towards evening the wind freshened and they were in motion again, smoothly and gently.

On Monday the 5th they were still running down the coast of Norway, but now at a greater distance, heading for Lindesnes in the extreme south. The shoreline could be seen, bare, lofty but level, with occasional heights inland. Ann sat on deck reading Shakespeare, and breaking off now and then to watch the changing scenery of the eastern horizon as the vessel sped past cape after cape.

But the gales returned and the poetic gave place to the most miserably prosaic. Another horrible night and day with no land in sight, and heavy seas. Ann was no brave sailor now. She sighed and moaned over her seasickness, her appalling head-aches and her flooded cabin. It does not appear that Nils was a patient comforter; he revelled in the roaring gale.

They came safely past Skagen, the northern tip of Denmark, then the island of Anholt, and sped under full sail towards Kullen on the Swedish coast. It was now that life began to smile once more. Ann strolled on deck with Nils '... this celestial evening when all is calm again, and with all our sails set, we are quietly dropping down on Kullen.'

The sun sank beyond the low shores of Jutland and there followed a light breeze from the west which flapped the canvas merrily and then flew swiftly on to Sweden, leaving the *Naiad* alone with the moon.

They did not reach Elsinore until two o'clock on Thursday the 8th. Captain Pålson rowed them ashore – 'Oh blessed and twice blessed land!' – and they had a good breakfast at the Hôtel du Nord, but Ann still felt too wretched to enjoy it. Little Elsinore had no attraction for her that day: it was a squalid transit-place, full of refuse and drinking-dens, with women looking like the Dutch – they ought then to have been charming! – and the old ones like Flemings. They had had a better view of Kronborg on the outward voyage, but even now it was an impressive sight, half fortress, half palace; so much at least Ann had to admit.

Soon they were at sea again, now off the Swedish coast, 'but very doucement'. They passed the island of Hven 'where the Swedes go to settle their affairs of honour', then Landskrona, as Elsinore vanished beyond the shining waters to the north and Copenhagen rose from the calm sea ahead. The whole Sound was full of vessels at rest, and soon the little *Naiad* too lay at anchor in the stillness of night.

But the wind rose and began beating at them, moaning and howling and driving rain before it. Ann was in despair. Captain Pålson was visited by the skipper of a schooner from Lisbon, laden with salt, and this man at once offered to have Ann rowed into Copenhagen if the weather next day was no better.

Next day dawned with adverse winds and rough water, and all the vessels scattered in search of shelter as they were unable to put to sea.

Poor Ann, they could not even row ashore for a hot meal. 'But those who have not money at command must learn wisdom by a life of contradiction.'

Monday the 12th was gloriously fine. The shining waters mirrored the sky, unruffled by the least little zephyr, but streaked here and there by seaweed drifting by. Hundreds of vessels of every imaginable kind spread their sails to dry, swinging at anchor in the strong current. Ann philosophizes on the virtue of Patience, and describes how she scraped together their last grains of salt for the soup – which Nils and the skipper ate with salt herring! Nils celebrated the sunny day by repacking his trunk, while Ann, to entertain skipper and crew, opened Mama's jewel-box and rearranged all the contents.

Next day the wind freshened a little, and once more they were southward bound. Copenhagen was left behind and it was not long before they were sweeping north towards Falster under a mild, grey sky with a following wind. Soon, soon!

But it was three o'clock on Thursday 15 October before they sailed past the end of Vallgatan, their own street in Karlskrona, and Ann was sure she could see Mama and Mary up there. Surely they must have heard the telegraph report from the fortress when the *Naiad* passed it two hours earlier? But she continues placidly with her travel-journal while awaiting The End. Once again the sea was choppy and unpleasant; once again she suffered seasickness and frustration. Her home was so near, so near, and yet out of reach.

Early on the morning of the 16th, a piercingly cold morning, the spires of Karlskrona reappeared and 'soon, soon we shall see Mama and Mary and our most beloved little angel. Oh God, how thankful I am – and we shall read the 107th Psalm together tonight, the voyagers' and mariners' Psalm, and thank Him for His mercy towards us.' Only two days before, an English brig and a sloop had been wrecked just off the fortress.

But it was pitch dark before they stepped ashore. Weary and impatient they battled against the wind along Drottninggatan, which seemed endless.

They found mother, sister and child all well, God be thanked.

Little Tuttan was sleeping on the sofa, her fair curls over her rosy cheeks – and how she had grown! She never woke until they were sitting at the dinner-table, which was beautifully adorned with flowers, and with silver that Mama had bought in their absence. The meal was delicious. Ann then slipped upstairs and into bed, and took Tuttan with her; but the baby cried and was shy, having forgotten her. Later tea was brought up to Ann, and the family talked till after midnight while Tuttan slept in her arms. The hours of night sped past, but neither Nils nor Ann could sleep; they seemed in a fever.

10

Family Life and Money Worries

THEY were up early next day, but Ann took a long time dressing: Tuttan had learnt so many new tricks that had to be admired. Immediately after breakfast Nils went to the customs house, and soon afterwards Petter and Anders brought home trunk after trunk. Unpacking could begin.

Thoughts and conversation dwelt on 'the journey' for a long time to come. It was the greatest fun to show and explain the contents of all the trunks to the stream of visitors, and to distribute presents. Mama had managed to pay off some of the debts, and had even made a temporary loan of 100 riksdollars banco to one of the former – and evidently somewhat insensitive – creditors. But what should Nils do but rush off with Dr Westring to look at an electrical machine which he soon hoped to call his own! There went another 100 RdB.

All the same, he was as eager as Mama to arrange all the furniture that had come, to unpack silver and linen, hang pictures and go through albums and portfolios of drawings and water-colours.

... we had a great varnishing-day with all the paintings, and when dinner came and we saw our work and our day's labour hanging around us, we felt as proud as if we were in a *real* art-gallery.

For they had brought old family portraits and many fine works of art from Scotland. There were the splendid portraits of Alexander and Mary Campbell, painted by Chinnery many years ago in Calcutta. There was a delightful one of cousin

Mary Phillips which her brother Henry had painted especially for Ann, also paintings by Thomas Phillips R.A. himself, and by the talented sisters Elisabeth and Mary, both of whom were skilled in drawing and water-colour.

Perhaps after all one could come to feel at home here in Sweden.

Those who most keenly rejoiced in this fine new home were Aunt Ulrique de Frese and her husband; though the book-cases which Nils had so promptly ordered from the most expensive cabinet-maker in the town were considered by the colonel to be quite unnecessary. He had the same opinion of the alarming quantities of foreign books they had brought with them. What, one wonders, were his views on Vörta Mill, which Mary Campbell brought that autumn. It cost 100,000 riksdollars banco, but was expected to prove a profitable investment.

Autumn came, with mild grey days. The apples in the orchard were picked, and more than one basketful passed through Ann's hands to be turned into *compote aux pommes*. Then the vegetables had to be brought in, and after that there had been

... a very horrid operation going on of killing of our four poor sheep somewhere on the premises, which makes us very careful of our regards as we go ... and in the evening the nurse made blood-puddings – horrid name – which they all delight in particularly.

Next came candle-making; Mama was down in the maids' room all day, making candles with them. The tallow – 100 lbs of it – had been purified under Nils' scientific supervision. Ann took no part in that process, nor in the candle-making, as she had only her fine silk morning gown, but she could twist the wicks. Was she really so spoilt and silly, or was the expected baby making her feel out of sorts? She complained a great deal about the cobbled streets of Karlskrona, and confessed in the middle of November that since her return she had been off the place only four times, and had no wish for further excursions. But the garden was lovely, and it seems that she did go as far as Hubendick's shop and came back with – an apron: '... a thing I do most thoroughly hate and detest, and which I shall now have for the first time.'

Was it Mama or Nils who insisted on it?

Ann also thought it a great nuisance to have guests in a house where the ladies themselves had to do the work, as evidently no competent housemaids or cooks were to be had in this country.

Thus our short days slip away unremarked by any save household events of small consequence. . . . I get up early, go to bed early or late according as I can keep my feet longer and am *greatly* occupied with keys, cupboards and servants.

Aunt de Frese called this 'managing one's économie'.

If Ann found it a drab existence, Nils must have found it equally dull, if not more so. He fitted up a laboratory for his experiments, and we know that he devised a simple and in-expensive method of purifying camphor. He patented it in Stockholm and wrote about it to his mother's brother Sebastian Gripenberg, in Finland, from whom he hoped for an introduction to some rich and enterprising Russian backer. We don't know whether he ever received an answer from his uncle.

But Nils also did his best to run his petticoat household. He scolded the maids – the lads, of course, were amenable – he wrote Sunday Reflections and read sermons to the domestics. He tried to cheer and amuse his ladies by reading aloud from Pelham and Eugene Aram: 'Vile morality beneath the fine style', Ann declared.

On 4 March another daughter was born. She was named Anne Elisabeth, but we know nothing more of her than that, as the last entry in Ann's journal is dated 15 November the previous year. There must have been great rejoicing, though the responsibility for his growing family must have borne heavily on Nils.

He seems not to have been in touch with any of his relatives except Aunt Ulrique; the others may have supposed that all must be well with him now that he had settled down comfortably with the wealth of the Indies at his disposal. It is true that sister Johanna was fabulously successful and making a great deal of money; but this money poured rapidly away owing to her mother's lavish mode of life and the optimism of their young cashier. In any case they were away in Naples at this time, and very far from everything in their homeland.

Perhaps Nils was doing his best to make an income, but his projects remained unrealized until he could find someone willing to back him. Also, Nils was a man of ideas. He had no patience and perhaps he lacked the ability to carry out all the projects of his fertile brain.

The next step was to sound the family in London in the matter of the red dye, which was said to be excellent, and at the same time induce Baring's Bank to release some of Mary Campbell's capital. Something had to be done, and it was decided that Nils should go to London. Crying children, nappies and lack of money cannot have been at all congenial to him; and being as usual convinced of ultimate success in all his ventures, he set forth.

The parting was sorrowful. There is a letter of his from Lübeck which seems moving in its grief – but was the grief genuine? Was he already planning a longer separation? He does not omit description of the notable sights of the city. In company with a friendly American party he visited the Marienkirche and climbed to the top of the spire: 360 stairs and another 150 up a ladder with rungs fifteen inches apart, as if Ann herself had recorded it in her journal, and from there the view was so overwhelmingly beautiful that he wept . . .

I thought of you, my dear, dear love. . . . I would have given the world for a kiss, yes I think I would have died on the spot had I only been permitted to throw my arms round you, my dearest beloved wife. I thought on all the troubles you will have now, and my heart was filled with bitterness. . . . O write to me, my own, my life, my dearest wife. I am now going to Hamburg. God bless you and preserve you. A thousand kisses for our two little angels. . . . God bless you all [here he made a cross] on that mark I have laid for you all I can, that is many kisses. Farewell, farewell and again farewell beloved wife.

> for ever yours
> Nils Gustaf.

It was 30 June 1836.

11

Flight to Freedom

NILS arrived in London after a passage of only forty-eight hours, in glorious weather. First he was to introduce himself to the family in Hanover Square, who were impatiently awaiting him: Ann's beloved Aunt Elisabeth, Uncle Thomas and the four Phillips cousins, whose home had become Ann's when she arrived there from India at the age of four. The thought that Nils and these dear people were now to meet was some consolation to her at parting from him; it was almost as if she herself had been able to come. She would hear every scrap of news – and none but Nils could tell a tale so vividly. By letter first, of course.

All went as Ann had hoped. The grand little house in Hanover Square opened its doors and its heart to him, and he won golden opinions. Both Aunt Elisabeth and the cousins sounded quite charmed: 'I am really half-inclined to envy you him. But without joking we all like him extremely,' wrote Cousin Mary. But they were greatly disappointed when he declined their invitation to stay with them while he was in London, and instead rented rooms which he shared with two travelling companions; rooms conveniently situated certainly, just round the corner, but still . . .

The trio were invited to dinner the very first day, and Aunt Elisabeth was much pleased with the polished manners and perfect English of one of the companions. He seemed very well read in English literature, both prose and poetry. This Captain Gosselman – that was his name, was it not? – seemed well-

informed and widely travelled. How widely travelled Captain
Carl August Gosselman in fact was, Aunt Elisabeth could not
know, but he was almost to be compared with her good friends
Cook and Franklin. On that occasion he could hardly have said
anything of the massive volumes he had published about his
travels in Colombia and North America, and certainly did not
mention that he was even then on his way to South America,
partly on government business. The third man of the party was
dismissed briefly and indignantly as 'a young cub . . . a poor
dumb creature who knows nothing but his Swedish'. But she did
not allow the cub to colour her ideas of Nils Gustaf; quite the
contrary. To give him the chance of making some useful contacts
she gave a dinner-party for him the following evening.

She writes a full account of this in a letter to Karlskrona.
Heading the list of guests were Sir Francis and Lady Chantrey;
perhaps Elisabeth was especially glad to show off someone who
was not only a famous sculptor and a legendary shot at wood-
cock, but also a truly *spirituel* and likeable party guest. Elisabeth
did not forget what her sister had written of brilliant Florentine
society, nor what she had been told of Nils Gustaf's interest in
chemistry and natural philosophy, so she invited the well-known
chemists Brande and Hatchet and the astronomer Baily. It was a
highly successful evening, but unfortunately she was never to see
any results from her kind efforts on Nils' behalf. Nils at any
rate did not exert himself, and preferred to run about with his
helpless 'cub'.

He had assured his charming relatives that he would spend
his days with them – so far as business allowed, of course. But
business proved extraordinarily time-consuming. Nils appeared
only briefly at breakfast before hastening to the City – and even
then not on his own account, but on that of his inopportune
compatriot. Elisabeth repeated her indignant comments on this
impossible young man who had gone out into the world without
knowing a word of any language but Swedish. He was now

pulling and pushing Nils hither and thither from morning till night, so that the family hardly caught a glimpse of their kinsman. Nils had certainly been a good Samaritan to him, and without his ungrudging and ceaseless efforts, it seemed, the wretched creature would have been lost. There was never time for any sensible conversation at the breakfast-table, beyond what concerned the next hour, and as to how and where he could make the best use of that time.

Their plans for showing him something of London were reduced to utter confusion. Nevertheless Nils contrived to see many fine things in company with his new cousins, and to meet a number of people. On 10 July he would be free at last; he had only to accompany his fellow-countryman to Portsmouth, and after that there would be no more bother with him. It was true that the fellow had tried to tempt Nils to go with him – had even offered to pay his passage to America – 'but do not be uneasy on that score, dear Ann. He so dearly loves his little wife and his little angels, and longs only for them.'

On 8 July Nils himself wrote to Ann and told her of his coming trip to Portsmouth, where he was to see his travelling-companion safely aboard. He hoped also to find a good market for oat-bran (from Vörta Mill). This was the only letter he sent her from London, though he knew she longed for news of him and for his impressions of Hanover Square. The handwriting runs free and clear, and the letter ends with tender words, with longing and with kisses: 'God bless you my life's flowers, Oh I sometimes feel so alone. . . . Now I wish to be back again, kiss my little, little loves.'

After that, silence. To the people in London Nils wrote, 'From Portsmouth I am going straight to Glasgow.' They thought this very odd, since the best route to Glasgow was via London. Nor did he say when he expected to return to them, which was extremely inconvenient as they had to make their own plans for the summer. They waited and they waited. Ann wrote to them rather anxiously, asking what they knew of Nils and his affairs. Aunt Elisabeth replied with some asperity that she expected Ann herself to answer that question, as no word had been received from Nils since his announcement of his strange expedition to Glasgow. She had assumed that by this time he was already back in Karlskrona and could give some explanation of his peculiar behaviour.

But he was gone. His relatives in London and Karlskrona were beside themselves with anxiety. Ann was the calmest, although she could find no other explanation for her husband's disappearance than that there had been some accident. As soon as it was known that Nils had not returned to Karlskrona, dear, patient Uncle Phillips left his fashionable sitters and began to make inquiries. In this connection a queer bill of exchange came to light, but in the end it was satisfactorily explained. 'What a relief to know that there was nothing fraudulent about it.'

In November came confirmation that Nils von Schoultz had never gone to Glasgow. Monteith and Hamilton, the industrialists there, who at the time of the agreeable young Swede's earlier visit had been encouraging and enthusiastic about his red dye, had certainly been in written communication with him quite recently, but had told him that unless the dye could be made more stable than it had proved at the latest test, they had no use for it. Messrs Monteith and Hamilton went on to say that they had explained to Mr de Schoultz that so far as the red dye was concerned his journey to Scotland would be a waste of time, but that if notwithstanding he chose to honour them with a visit he would be most welcome.

The Portsmouth agent was able to inform Uncle Phillips that a passenger had bought a ticket for America at the last minute. His name was unknown, as was that of the other gentleman, but both were thought to be Swedes. No unfranked letters had been found at any of the addresses given; this was established by careful inquiry at any number of post offices. Between London and Sweden letters sped in quick succession; from America came not a word.

Ann's faith in Nils remained unshaken. Cousin Mary Phillips wrote:

I like and I admire extremely your noble and continuous confidence in your husband. . . . My feelings are the same as yours, that Nils has but rashly, yet *most* rashly, undertaken the journey in desperate hope of doing or gaining something to set you all free at once.

Time passed, and silence fell upon his name.

12

Soldier of Fortune in the New World

ONCE again Nils had been tempted; once again adventure
beckoned and he followed without hesitation – or at least he
stifled any warning voice. A desperate man finds it easy to gag
his conscience, and there is no doubt that Nils was driven to
extremity. He could not return to Sweden empty-handed. His
red dye was no better than raspberry-juice. The milled oats from
Vörta were good for nothing but fisherman's porridge and there
was no money to be made out of anything.

And who could force him back into the treadmill now that he
was free at last? Nothing venture, nothing win.

For him, as always, to decide was to act; but this time the
decision was born of desperation. He had courage but little
patience. Once more he found his true element in the renewed
prospect of departure, freedom and a voyage to unknown destina-
tions. He was (and remained) a rash gambler. Though he may
have dreamt of love, it was hardly of the temperate kind which
was all his childlike little Ann could offer him – and certainly
not in a ménage involving mother- and sister-in-law, the obligations of head of the household, and a fenced-in, bourgeois existence. He saw no sense in toiling to pay off half-forgotten,
paltry little debts. Debts of honour vanished from his memory
like melting snow.

Yet one wonders whether this journey was quite as spon-
taneous as it seemed. Nils Gustaf was certainly familiar with
C. D. Arfvedson's book about his travels in the North American States, and would have recalled his description of salt-

production in Syracuse; that lucrative trade which might be made even more profitable by the introduction of new methods, similar to his own in camphor-refining.

Then Captain Gosselman came on the scene, and who knows whether, all unawares, he may have added fuel to the flames? Like thousands before him, Nils Gustaf cast loose from a clogging past, and headed for the New World and its boundless opportunities.

On 13 August 1836 (or, as another version has it, the 18th) the traveller stepped ashore from the vessel *Ocmulgee*. His silent companion was and remains unknown, having vanished from the scene after buying the tickets and walking up the gang-plank at Portsmouth. *Ocmulgee*'s passenger-list shows 'N. G. von Schoultz, Army Officer, aged 28'. There is another name, Loethman, which may be that of a Swede.

It was a serious, purposeful man who walked off the boat, and he wasted no time. He did not need to go further than the great warehouses, in which goods from the interior were stacked up awaiting shipping, to find out where the saltworks were. There lay his real future.

There was constant traffic along the salt-route between Syracuse and New York City: he could sail up the Hudson in one of the salt-boats returning empty, and take the stage-coach on to Syracuse. It was no speedy journey, certainly, but as he sailed peacefully up the mighty river he wrote up his journal and pondered his coming encounter with salt. It had been the Indians who first discovered the salt springs and carried on a primitive form of distillation, but the white men when they came soon took spring after spring away from them. The first one to be exploited was that of Salina, which at that time was nothing more than a large pit, twenty foot square by thirty deep. The water from it was drawn up in great cauldrons and evaporated, leaving the salt deposit behind.

Salt was transmuted into money. The news spread and settlers poured in from far and wide. Every man became a salt-boiler, with his own pump to raise the brine. The springs seemed inexhaustible, the salt extracted like white gold. Something of an early Klondyke grew up around the once peaceful twin centres of Salina and Syracuse; for here was a staple product for which there was an almost unlimited demand. Soon more than sixty boileries were sending up their smoke. Among the giant hickories, elms, and maples of the vast forests, axe and saw rang out – though faintly, drowned by the roar of fires that burned day and night under the vats.

Salt was shipped out in huge quantities; woods thinned and gave place to cultivated fields. The hastily-hewn log cabins of the salt-boilers became farm-houses on well tended farms. Where ruthless tree-felling had destroyed the forests, open vats were constructed for evaporating salt in the sun. So it went on; but although both boileries and open vats produced salt in great quantities, new methods of increasing and improving the yield were still being sought.

To this land of opportunity came Nils Gustaf. He surveyed the installations and learned of the drawbacks in existing processes. What was needed was a more efficient method of purifying brine. Soon he had set up his laboratory and started his experiments. The tough salt-boilers, being of the same enterprising breed as himself, took both the foreign chemist and his projects seriously.

He was thus able to put his attainments to the test, and very soon he believed he had discovered a considerably simpler method of purifying the water than the one then in use. In the spring of 1837 one of the many boileries adopted his new process, and when it proved satisfactory he decided to take out a patent for the invention.

On his journey south to Washington, he seems to have passed through not only the states of New York and Maryland, but to have visited also the salt-producing centres of Pennsylvania,

Kentucky and Virginia. He aroused people's interest every-where, and his refining-process was found to be particularly suited to the waters of the Kanawha River. Many offers were made him, and contracts were drawn up, to be completed as soon as he returned with his patent. Castles in the air towered up in a haze of gold, and gold would soon fill his pockets . . . Suddenly we find him in Baltimore, writing to Ann. Had he written earlier? Perhaps more than once? Had Ann written to him, and if so to what address?

Two almost identical letters have been preserved, copied out in Ann's clear handwriting and headed: 'Copy of the two last and the first I ever received from N. G. von Schoultz, after his sailing for America, July 1836.'

Baltimore the 1st June 1837

Dearly Beloved Anna!

I write in a great hurry from this place, because I think that however little the enclosed vexel [bill of exchange] is, it may be of use to you. May God grant it to come into your hands. I could find no remittance either on Sweden or London in consequence of the unfortunate money-trouble now in America; I therefore was forced to send you this one on Amsterdam (Holland) on the house of *Jacob Sigrist* given out here by Mr C. *Heincken & Schumacher*. Oh my dear wife! how horrid my situation is, occasioned by the uncertainty as to you and our children. Not a single word have I got from you. I know, my dearest that if you are still spared for my happiness, your fault it cannot be, but must have arisen from my constant changing place here. Yet after the orders I have left in the State of New York, Virginia, Maryland etc., I ought to have at least one letter. Almighty God! how I have prayed for your life, my dear, my own Anna – but I will not think of this now. My heart be-comes oppressed, and sorrow consumes the strength I have need of to finish my prosperous undertaking in the United States. I return today again through Washington to Kanawha in Virginia, to settle with [the] Company there. They have now bought a right to use my discovery in their works for $25,000 or a hundred thousand of our Riksdollar. At the State of New York they are anxiously waiting for me. They will pay me in that State $50,000 or two hundred thousand Riksdollar. After having finished there I have promised to start the works in the States of Massachusetts, Pennsylvania, Ohio, Kentucky, Tennessee, Alabama and Illinois.

About the 1st of next month I will send to Mr Phillips in London a remittance for you to pay all our debts and then I will also begin to send you by separate posts money until you have one hundred thousand Riksdollar, which you my own and dearly beloved Anna will accept for your pinmoney. Great God! perhaps you are gone, but no I won't believe it.

Before you get this I will again be in the State of New York, wherefore you must address your letters: *United States, Salina, Onondago County, N.Y.*

For God's sake do not forget to address in that order. The lowest two letters (N.Y.) signifies that it is in the State of New York that the place is situated.

I send one letter enclosed to Mr Jacob Sigrist, Amsterdam, so that you may get either this one or the other. Ask Palander and he will help you in this.

God bless you, dearest love, and our dearest children; my love to Mamma and Mary.

When I send the money to Mr Phillips I will send you some volumes of my journal and correspondence here. You will see it was written for you.

God bless you and protect you. I kiss the letter thousand thousand times, and send them to you. I would give more than I can express to see you one moment, to embrace you one moment, to hear your voice one moment. *Farväl, farväl.* Your ever affectionate husband
N. von Schoultz.

Both letters, then, had arrived in Karlskrona by 1 July 1837. Ann gave thanks to God who had so tried her trust in Nils, and who by this token of Nils' fidelity had restored her will to live, and given her fresh strength to bear whatever further burdens he thought fit to lay upon her shoulders.

To the glaring discrepancy between the thousands of dollars

boasted of by Nils in these letters and the paltry £150 he actually sent her she gave not a thought. The future was radiant. Even her relatives in London forgave him all their anxiety on his account, their endless inquiries, their grief and sleepless nights.

Yet neither letter nor money ever reached Mr Phillips, nor was any further sign of life received by the family in Sweden.

What did it all mean? What convincing explanation is to be found? How sincere was Nils in what he wrote? How far did he himself believe in those brilliant prospects? His letters were dated 1 June from Baltimore – yet two days earlier he had applied, in Washington, for American citizenship! Of this there is no word, no hint, in what he wrote. Naturalization may have been necessary for the registration of his patent and to assure his future on American soil. Did he picture such a future for himself alone, without Ann?

In *Records of Declarations of Intentions for Naturalizations in the District of Columbia* the following entry was later found: 'On 30th May 1837, in Washington, the Swedish subject Nils Scholtewskii von Schoultz, aged 39 [!] made application for American citizenship. He was a resident of N.Y., where he had arrived on 13th of April [*sic*] from London.'

What are we to make of this, and of the letters? Was this Nils Scholtewskii identical with Nils Gustaf, or was he someone else? No, it must have been one and the same man, though from that time onwards he always signed himself S. von Schoultz. He also became a little vague as to his nationality, and had no objection to being regarded as a Pole: one Polish refugee among so many others. His great-great grandfather had possessed estates in Lithuania, his great-great grandmother had been Polish, and he himself had fought for Polish freedom.

And the letters? If he had not written before, why now? Had he made the whole story up merely to deceive – to make a final floodlit appearance before vanishing for ever? Despair cries out from those letters, and only a man driven to extremity could have devised such fantasies. May it not rather be that success, whether real or imagined, had induced the adventurer to jettison all reason, all responsibility? Freedom, that wild and reckless freedom that goes with gold, and with gold alone, tempted him to deny his past. Nothing should hinder him now that at last he was heading for fortune. *Was schert mich Weib! Was schert mich Kind!*

Then suddenly, perhaps, he perceived with horror the treachery of these secret designs of his, and fled panic-stricken in the hope of a passage to Europe. But no. The die was cast. Easing his conscience with the £150, he headed south again.

A new man under a new name.

He passed through Virginia, again riding zig-zag as if following the course of hidden streams, and halting where the salt springs emerged. He inspected the most important of them and analysed their waters. He did business, or at least made contacts. He felt at home in the South, where cultured people of French descent made him welcome. A certain Mr McCombie offered him one of his farms, which he bought – or accepted in payment of a gambling-debt. It is stated in another connection that the place was called Salt Rock and that its owner was William McComus, a lawyer. Nils told them all that when he had fulfilled certain obligations in the North, he would return and settle down for good among his charming, carefree friends in the South. No one here asked who, whence or why; his French accent was recommendation enough, being a slightly old-fashioned and courtly one, dating from the days of Lafayette and von Fersen. M. de Schoultz was welcome everywhere, and was agreed by all to be an acquisition to society. He could repeat the latest gossip from Europe. He appreciated a well-composed menu and – but this was only whispered – he could both win and lose with grace. Unfortunately he always went away before the last word was spoken. In that art too he was a past-master.

But could anyone guess at the impact made on that foreigner by those soft, deep voices speaking to him in their languid cadence? Such had been the shy, hesitant voice of a young girl in Florence, years ago. He would have liked to stay – but he must move on.

On his return to friendly little Salina, Nils Gustaf seems to have had little to relate of his experiences during his months of absence; but there were others willing enough to talk. A man so unlike the general run of people in the neighbourhood aroused curiosity by his mere presence there. His background was evidently so different from theirs, and his grave, politely reserved behaviour in such contrast to that of the burly, loud-mouthed salt-boilers that these neighbours of his were bound to wonder where he had come from, and why. Old Europe was a world so distant in space and time that he might as well have dropped from the moon.

But rumour? Rumour floats across oceans and continents, by-passing well-obliterated trails.

One such travellers' tale concerned a man who had been in company with an enchanting young singer and her two brothers, in Florence. They were Swedes, and poor, as distinguished persons of the day often were; and one of the young gentlemen had married a rich Scottish lady. His description tallied – and yet it did not: Mr von Schoultz was a Pole and had been in the States for a long time. It was a curious story, but no doubt there was some adequate explanation. And indeed, Mr von Schoultz had heard that a cousin of his had recently arrived in America – a cousin who bore exactly the same name as himself! On previous occasions he had felt constrained to draw people's attention to this annoying circumstance, and it was for this reason – among others – that he had now added the ancient name of his family to his own.

Why all these explanations? Had he invented this cousin? Not entirely. In Finland there was indeed a cousin named Nils, born in 1805 and christened Constantin Nils Lorentz von Schoultz, but he called himself Constantin only. He too had been at the storming of Warsaw, but outside the walls with a Russian regiment. He had been decorated with the *Virtuti Militari* among other distinctions, and had been presented with the gold half-sabre for valour. He long survived as patriarch of the Finnish branch of the family; the events of his life are documented and well-known to all his kinsmen. Nils would have been aware that this cousin had been transferred to the infantry with the rank of major, and that he was now inspector of the military hospital in Helsinki (Helsingfors). An exceedingly respectable and conscientious citizen. After this time his journeys never extended beyond St Petersburg and Moscow, and he could therefore never have given rise to any American rumours.

But such gossip never bothered the good folk of Salina: they were not so petty. This interesting chemist was welcome everywhere and won friends everywhere; in this place he seemed to have found a field of activity that suited him, and people who welcomed him into their circle and hoped to keep him there. The German colony adopted him as a son, Pole though he might be; yet he attached himself to a hospitable family of English descent.

In the company of Warren Green, a pleasant and cultivated young property-owner, and his delightful sister Mrs Emeline Field, Nils found an atmosphere that was familiar and dear to him. With them he could talk of his past, yet they too were convinced that this melancholy man was Polish. The border-line between fantasy and reality in his stories is difficult to determine. The language may have given rise to misunderstanding, for it was mentioned later that 'he had only an imperfect knowledge of English' when he first arrived in the country. He had lost his fortune, his family was scattered, his marriage hopelessly wrecked. Emeline Field knew what loneliness was, having been herself recently widowed. Hearing her talk, he could not but think of another lonely and unhappy young woman. There was no peace for him here.

In the summer of 1838 he went south again 'to inspect his properties in Kanawha'. When at the end of the summer he returned he encountered a mysterious, silent unease everywhere. It had existed before he left, but now there was menace in it.

13

Fire Over Canada

As early as 1837, when Nils Gustaf returned from his long
trip to Washington, he had been met everywhere by excited
rumours and an unexplained feverish tension. The rumours came
from Canada; their theme was the arbitrary and oppressive rule
of the British, and the indifference of the government in London
to the lamentable conditions in this distant part of the realm.
In vain had the Canadians made proposals and pleaded for
rational reform: nothing was done. The Americans were only
too ready to believe the worst about 'poor, enslaved Canada', for
in recent times thousands of Canadians – 80,000 in seven years
– had crossed the border and settled in the neighbouring States.
These emigrants kept in touch with their homes and embellished
the rumours with accounts of their own recent sufferings. The
junta in power over there – the Family Compact – had by its
arrogance and self-seeking reduced the whole country to desperation.

There was some basis for these rumours. The wife of a
high-ranking official in Upper Canada described in a diary her
gloomy observations in the years before 1837. Rocking in her
canoe on the Detroit river she noted the gay bustle and activity
on the American shore, in contrast to the Canadian side where
all was silent and deserted, bearing every sign of stagnation,
neglect and despair, as she wrote. A farmer's son from Vermont
had also much to tell of his travels in Canada. He was working
with a tanner of morocco leather in Watertown, but had made
many journeys between Toronto and Montreal, 'buying hides

133

and selling morocco', and had thus been able to observe conditions in Canada. Everywhere, he declared, he had had to listen to the inhabitants' bitter complaints of the rule they lived under. He minced no words on the subject of British sovereignty in Canada. Stories like this were eagerly listened to.

The free Americans were indignant. Could they in honour stand idly by while Human Rights were trampled underfoot by Tyranny, on their own continent? Small local newspapers south of the frontier outdid one another in news from 'reliable sources'. The same journals were then taken over to the Canadian side, and added fuel to the flames. They reported that in the east, too, in predominantly French-speaking Lower Canada, rebellion was in full swing. Father Louis Joseph Papineau, with fanatical ardour, brandished his banner and uttered the warcry of *'Vive la Nation Canadienne!'*, preaching revolt against 'the British, those latecome invaders'. In Upper Canada, the region nearest the salt springs, the pro-reformers had acquired an uninvited adherent and self-appointed leader, 'William Lyon Mackenzie, a stupid, ambitious and quarrelsome journalist'.

And now something really had begun to happen in Canada. The whole frontier region, including Onondaga County, was set ablaze. Honest American citizens, often the best in their communities, sold their property and scraped money together to support 'the patriots'. In vain the government in Washington warned its nationals against infringing the pact of neutrality, being most unwilling to damage its relations with Britain all over again, when at last after so much mutual bitterness a *modus vivendi* had been achieved. Yet appeals came in – from Canada, it was said – for armed assistance. Recruiting and weapon-training began.

Some time in May, during Nils Gustaf's absence, a certain Mr Estebrook from Cleveland, Ohio, had come to Watertown, which was not far from Salina, and founded a secret society or lodge for the liberation of Canada. A number of other such lodges were established in different places and with different aims and objects. Hunters' Lodge was the one designed to liberate the town of Prescott and Fort Wellington on the north shore of the St Lawrence. Preparations were secret. The foreigner was absorbed in his own affairs until he set forth on his travels again, and for the time being remained outside all the activity in his new home town.

New and perturbing rumours kept pouring in from Canada. The fact that the British government was sincerely willing to meet the young Canadian provinces half-way had no effect on the situation. They were given a large measure of self-determination, and governors of their own choice. The Canadians themselves held conflicting views as to what they wanted; they fought each other savagely, and either the wrong man was put in authority, or the newly-appointed governor did not receive support from London when he most needed it. It was said afterwards that the Rebellion of 1837–8 was a classic example of the damage that can be caused by the ambition, vanity and vindictiveness of individual men.

Both Papineau and Mackenzie were such men, and they would have nothing to do with moderate reforms. They wanted revolt, and they fanned the flames. Clashes occurred, with a greater or lesser amount of bloodshed, but the two heroes took care to remain unscathed. So far no one in the States doubted their assurances that Canada was now ripe for the final conflict, and Americans in their thousands joined the ranks of the freedom movement, selling and mortgaging their land to finance the enterprise. Canadians south of the border joined up and were promised land wherever they chose in the north, after victory was won. They knew – everyone knew – that Generals Mackenzie and Birge were mustering their forces.

On his return to Salina from Kanawha in the late summer of 1838, Nils Gustaf found that he was impatiently awaited, for he if anybody must be won over to the cause of liberty and human rights. A certain Mr Stone called upon him, and soon initiated him into what was going on. This seems to have been Mr Erasmus Stone, the post-master of Salina, who was regarded as the leading liberal of the place. He had furthermore been branded by orthodox Presbyterians as frivolous and unseemly in his conduct. He did not keep the Sabbath day holy; he visited dance halls, and worked in his garden on Sundays. He now told Nils Gustaf of the preparations along the border and in the immediate neighbourhood; of Hunters' Lodge in Syracuse; of the bullets cast at night for a coming attack on Prescott; and he declared that no self-respecting citizen of New York State would rest until the banner of liberty had been presented to his Canadian brothers.

Such storm signals were familiar to von Schoultz; were they as welcome now as before? He seems not to have hesitated for a moment, but to have dived headlong into the adventure. He had fought for Poland, though in vain, and he was still ready to sacrifice the last drop of his blood in the cause of freedom. Did he ever think of Finland? He now figured as a Pole, and the addition of the ancient name of Scholtewskii to his own appeared to him as having been a prophetic sign. No doubt he forgot that it was most usually spelt Czultecki; it was of no real importance. He was S. von Schoultz.

People must certainly have been eager to enrol a man of Nils Gustaf's military attainments and experience, writes one of the many authors who described his share in the uprising.

But if Nils von Schoultz had not been a true lover of liberty he would never have joined his fortunes with those of the Hunters. He was a successful inventor, he owned property in the South and in New York State, he had gained loyal friends in both regions, and he had won the love of the beautiful and congenial sister of his boon companion. Only an over-whelming conviction of the justice of the cause and his own obligation to act in its behalf could have moved him.

He swore the sacred oath of the fighters for liberty. Or did he? At his trial he denied having done so.

I swear to do my utmost to promote Republican institutions and ideas throughout the world – to cherish them, to defend them. . . . I pledge my life, my property and my sacred honour to the Association. . . . I promise until death, that I will attack, combat and help to destroy . . . every power or authority of Royal origin upon this continent. . . . So help me God.

He accompanied the senior officers of the Lodge on a tour, and everywhere he met confederates, including Canadian revolutionaries, who vowed 'that the workers in their country, its militia and the British troops stationed there would unite to crush the despotism of the detested Tory aristocrats as soon as forces from the United States had landed on their soil'.

He hastened to New York City, where he knew of Polish refugees as ardent as himself for the cause of liberty. For a time he maintained a recruiting-office, 'a regular office, 300 Pearl Street, New York', where volunteers could join. Some of them remembered fighting beside him within the walls of Warsaw, and he appears to have paid the passage of a number of them. His activities were commented upon in a letter to Europe, and later in the American press, as provocation inspired by the Czar! He spoke no Polish, as he said himself, while his secretary affirmed that he did. After a while he returned to Salina, where events were moving towards a climax.

The prelude to the final tragedy of the Canadian revolt was dramatic enough. After many mishaps, Mackenzie had begun quietly running arms into Canada, to a small town in the Niagara region. The British captured his little steamer *Caroline*, emptied her and sent her down the river in flames. She sank before reaching the Falls, yet the story of how the burning vessel plunged over and was smashed in the thundering waters was told far and wide.

On the night of 29/30 May 1838 the British steamer *Sir*

Robert Peel was quite pointlessly set on fire, though not until passengers and crew and their belongings had been put ashore. To cries of 'Remember *Caroline!*' the vessel was attacked by fanatics dressed and painted like Indians, among them the notorious Bill Johnson with his belt stuck full of knives and pistols. After this exploit he styled himself 'Commodore of the Canadian Republic'. The whole affray has been called a splendid example of private enterprise. But the final drama began on 11 November 1838.

Many hundred volunteers, mostly young, decent farmers, had been assembling in the small towns south of the St Lawrence River and Ontario. Here they awaited orders from the Canadian leaders who had called them to arms in the name of liberty and justice.

Among those ready to obey those orders was Nils Gustaf, though he can no longer have shared the extravagant optimism expressed in the speeches of his comrades-in-arms. No one could have failed to notice how vague the orders were; they were borne on the wind, no one knew from whom. According to one source, von Schoultz had prepared a proper plan for the assault on Prescott, but General Birge flatly rejected it. This officer still lurked unseen, it seemed, behind the equally invisible thousands of his Canadian army. Yet the universal mood of confidence was unshaken. The assembly-point was to be Ogdensburg; here the leaders were waiting and here definite orders would at last be issued. Nils Gustaf bought tickets to Ogdensburg for himself and 'his servant Frederick Meals', as did the other thirty-four volunteers from Onondaga County.

The departure was celebrated by a solemn banquet in Salina, at which von Schoultz was presented with a valuable gift from his friends: a sword with a beautifully wrought hilt of silver. He also received a standard, a personal gift from the ladies, where on a blue silk ground an eagle rose on powerful wings towards a radiant star. Beneath this, embroidered in silk, were the words: *Liberated by the Onondaga Hunters*. He himself was to carry this victorious greeting from a hundred women on the shore of liberty to their oppressed sisters across the river. Nils himself declares that he was given the flag by Mr Stone, for presentation to General Birge.

On taking his leave he is said to have thanked his deeply moved companions 'for the friendship they had given a foreigner, who now bade them remember him as an unfortunate man whom they had comforted, a homeless man whom they had cherished as a kinsman'. Someone now begged him to sing for them, and he did so, ending with a little song of which he had written the words. The words were Swedish, and were later printed in one of the pamphlets describing the tragic affair at Windmill Point.

In this song he addresses a young woman from whom he now parts with a heavy heart, begging her to forgive the destiny which had brought him into her tranquil life, and to forgive him for causing her such sorrow now. That was all; but he had every reason to ask forgiveness. It is mentioned in several places as a well-known fact that 'von Schoultz was betrothed to a young lady in the neighbourhood'. We know that her name was Emeline Pech, and that she most probably belonged to the German colony in Onondaga. Although he did not consider himself as one of that coterie, he was often seen among them and was always welcome. From another source we hear that he was 'betrothed' to starry-eyed Emeline Field, 'contingent possibly on annulment of his previous marriage, for Nils was a devout Roman Catholic'.

More entanglements? With or against his will? The little ditty in the foreign language which no one understood makes no promises and declares no love. Pity and pity only rings true in that artless song, and she to whom the words of farewell were addressed could not suspect how oddly cool and unfeeling they sound.

Dared this calamitous man really dream of starting life all over again? With whom had he meant to share his future among the charming people of Virginia? Was someone waiting for him there too – someone to whom he had promised more than he could perform?

Was he clutching at this Canadian adventure, consciously or unconsciously, as an escape – a desperate cutting of the Gordian knot? Questions and more questions, but no answers.

14

Battle at the Mill

THE group of volunteers who set off with Ogdensburg as their goal were never allowed to land there. They were met by a message ordering them to proceed immediately to the Canadian side, where they would find officers and reinforcements. These were greatly needed, for in Sackett Harbour where men from the country round Watertown had assembled and had waited for a long time in vain, doubts were growing, and five or six hundred men had turned their backs on the bungled enterprise and returned to their homes. The remaining four hundred went aboard the steamer *United States*. They touched at Cape Vincent to pick up more 'patriots': simple folk in lumber-jackets and with little baggage. Further on, near Ogdensburg, they came up with two schooners which they took in tow by lashing them one on each side of the steam-boat. These vessels were heavily laden with men, arms and ammunition. As the *United States* steamed up the night-black St Lawrence, the ringing of church-bells and the beat of drums could be heard from Prescott, on the Canadian side. The patriots' expedition was no longer a secret from the British.

There are many almost identical accounts of these fateful days and nights, and some – perhaps the later ones – go in for picturesque detail.

At sunrise, just after the steamer had left Ogdensburg without anyone being allowed to land, one of the 'leaders', the notorious Bill Johnson, came aboard. He was bedecked in a war-like manner with pistols and knives, and he bellowed at his men to take possession of the vessel. Foster, the pilot, was compelled with a pistol at his head to remain at the wheel. Suddenly the magnificent General J. Ward Birge made his appearance, and the steamer headed for the Canadian shore.

But the British commandant in Kingston had no intention of permitting a landing, and despatched a timely gunboat, which opened fire on the *United States*. The third round went straight through the wheelhouse, decapitating the unfortunate pilot.

A few moments afterwards, when an orderly hastened below to request orders from the General, he found this officer 'stretched upon a mattress which was supported by eight or ten dining-room chairs, deathly pale and so badly shocked by a glimpse of the pilot's headless body that he could not speak'.

Few people ever had a chance to behold the gold-braided and hitherto eloquent 'General Officer Commanding Land Forces'. He stayed down there in the dining-saloon, treating a stomach-disorder as sudden as it was violent with powerful doses from the wine-cupboard; though he recovered enough to trumpet forth his extreme displeasure at the situation. He had counted upon far greater support. The troublesome stomach-upset compelled him to withdraw from the action, and he vanished into the darkness without rescinding any of his orders. The self-styled 'Commodore of the Fleet of the Republic of Canada' seems to have been of the opinion that his function was limited to vessels afloat, and did not include landings. He too contrived to disappear without cancelling any orders, and the unsuspecting patriots continued on their way through darkness and a snow storm.

The gunboat had vanished after completing her task, and on nearing the Canadian shore the schooners were cast loose from the steamer. The utmost confusion reigned as men and weapons were hustled ashore, whereupon the vessel slid away into the darkness.

There was no sign of either generals or Canadian troops,

it was a subdued little party that groped its way to some place where it might await further orders – or perhaps even the still invisible General Birge.

A participant who survived the events, Captain Wright, described them thus:

On Monday morning the 11th [November] we came in sight of Prescott; here the schooners were cut loose from the steamboat, and I embarked in one of them. Near Prescott they both ran aground – the schooner in which I was got clear and proceeded to Windmill Point, where we landed. Windmill Point is situated upon an elevated spot of ground on the brink of the St Lawrence, about one mile and a half below Prescott. The walls of the mill being shot proof, we made it our stand, and upon its summit floated our blue standard. The evening of the 11th was spent in making arrangements for the morrow; the schooner, which was aground in the morning, now proceeded to land her arms and munitions, but the greater part of the balls and other necessaries were left amid the confusion which prevailed. All our general officers had deceived us save Colonels von Schoultz, Woodruff and Abbey, who at first held but minor situations. After a deliberate consultation we elected von Schoultz to the post of Commander-in-Chief of our Patriot army, which had dwindled down from one thousand to two hundred souls; many of the soldiers, following the example of their superiors, had deserted us, and were talking (with their *extinguished* officers) bravely and gallantly in the streets of Ogdensburg.

The gentleman who now had command was brave and daring to a fault, and equal to any emergency. His height was five feet eleven; with firm and graceful limbs, with a well-bred gentleness in his manners, and an eye which blazed in its own liquid light. It was very rarely he smiled, but when he did it was as sunshine through prison bars; with a kind heart and as noble a soul as ever was found in fetters of clay, he was one whose very faults 'leaned towards virtue's side'. Our Spartan band consisted of two hundred men, for as the dross flees from the gold by fire, so the craven in soul and cowards in heart fled from the support of the cause of liberty in its hour of danger, even before the defence was commenced; and the blood of those who fell yet dye the garments of the false-hearted cowards that I have already mentioned.

About midnight, Bill Johnson came over in an open boat and informed us that five hundred men would join us before daylight. He was a messenger from those who not only had deserted us, but now wished to beguile by hopes that they too well knew would never be realized. This night no eye was closed, no hand was idle, and no heart was faint; all was hurry, bustle and confusion – all anxiety and expectation. In view of the expected reinforcement, we took possession of three stone out-buildings, weakening our force within the mill. The sun rose clear and cloudless – not one wave dimpled the waves of the St Lawrence, and above it curled a silver veil of mist as incense to the sky. Von Schoultz hailed the dawn as a good omen of the glorious sun-burst of Canadian liberty, but many an eye which gazed that morning upon the resplendent orb of light, ere night had closed for ever.

At nine o'clock a.m. three British steamboats came down from Prescott, anchoring opposite the mill, and opened a fire of balls and bomb-shells; at the same time, fifteen hundred of the Canadian militia and regulars made their appearance, the 83rd regiment occupying the centre and the militia forming the right and left wings. They were formed three deep when in line of battle. We formed likewise a line of battle, each man spreading from two to three yards apart, so as to cover their front, protected on three sides by walls and stone buildings and the river, whose steep banks prevented the shot and shells thrown by the enemy's marine from doing us any mischief, which passed above our heads and created death and disaster among their own land forces. . . . Our orders were not to fire a gun until we had received an assault from the British . . .

Von Schoultz too gives a brief account of these fateful days. He states that the men who had chosen him to be their leader at first asked him to take them back to the United States, but:

. . . we had then not a single boat for use, and the British steamer *Experiment* kept up a vigilant look-out on the river.

Tuesday morning we were attacked by land and water, at about seven o'clock; the firing ceased at three o'clock in the afternoon,

Nils Gustaf von Schoultz: a portrait from an ivory painting dated 1838, the year he was hanged. (Ontario Archives)

Top: The great square in Kuopio, Finland, showing the provincial governor's residence and the judge's house. Nils Gustaf von Schoultz, son of the judge, was born there in 1807. (Finnish National Museum)

Above: Viopaala: the Finnish manor house which was the home of Nils Gustaf's mother's family. Detail of a pencil drawing by M. V. Wright. (Finnish National Museum)

Top right: Polish patriots: 'Our blood, our gold, for Poland's freedom!' Nils Gustaf took part in the heroic defence of Warsaw, was captured by the Russians but escaped. Painting by an unknown artist. (Deutsche Phototek, Dresden)

Middle right: The von Schoultz family in Stockholm. The couple at the spinet are believed to be Nils Gustaf and his sister Johanna. Painting by an unknown artist of the 1820s. (From the collection of Mabel von Schoultz)

Bottom right: Florence by moonlight. Nils Gustaf fell in love with a Scots girl, Ann Campbell, whom he married there in 1834. (Wood engraving by G. Bauernfeinde, from *Italy: a wayfarer from the Alps to Etna*)

Above: A page from Ann's diary, which forms one of the main sources for this book

Top right: Angelica Catalani, the Italian singer, friend of Ann Campbell and Johanna von Schoultz. It was at her house that Ann and Nils Gustaf met

Bottom right: Karlskrona in Sweden, with the Admiralty clock tower in the background. Here Nils Gustaf and Ann spent their brief life together. Photographed in the 1880s. (Blekinge Museum, Sweden)

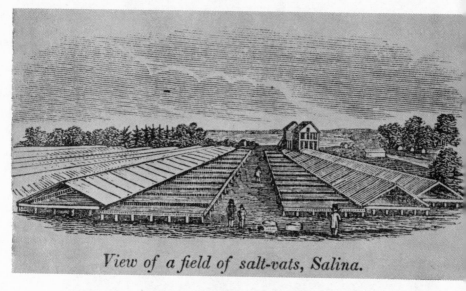

View of a field of salt-vats, Salina.

Top: The salt-extracting industry at Salina, where Nils Gustaf went to find his fortune in the New World. (From Barber and Howe: *Historical Collections of the State of New York*, 1841)

Above: Windmill Point on the St Lawrence river, scene of the idealistic attack on Upper Canada led by Nils Gustaf

Top: Nils Gustaf's grave at Fort Henry, Ontario
Above: Vorta Mill, Blekinge, Sweden. Drawing by Ann von Schoultz.
After her desertion and the news of her husband's death she lived in the
country with her two small daughters. (Family collection)

John A. Macdonald. The lawyer who defended Nils Gustaf in 1838, he was to become the first Prime Minister of Canada (Ontario Archives)

when the British withdrew and left us in our position. I had, during
the night, sent a man across the river on a plank, for boats. Tuesday
evening the general's adjutant came over, telling me a schooner would
be over to take us away. We carried our wounded down on the
bank, and waited with anxiety for the arrival of the vessel, but none
arrived. Wednesday passed away, and the British began to surround
us with considerable forces, harassing our flanks continually. I think,
Thursday night a steamer from the American shore approached us,
and we were informed by a couple of men sent ashore that it was
to take us away. We again carried out our wounded, but some few
rifle-shots of the British frightened the cowards away, and we were
again left to ourselves.

Friday, at about mid-day, a parley came from the British, for the
purpose of taking away the killed that lay on the field, and I delivered over to him the British wounded I had taken up, as I had
no medical stores of any kind, and it would have been a base and
unmanly policy to augment the sufferings of the wounded enemy.

The British emissary took back with him a brief note from
von Schoultz to the Commandant of the Forces of the Queen
in Prescott;

I am sending herewith two of your wounded, as I am unable to afford
them the care of which they are in need. In return I beg you to
receive my own wounded with kindness. If you can affirm upon your
honour that we are not regarded by the people here as their deliverers,
it will be for you to put an end to further bloodshed.

The white flag that was later flown was disregarded by the
British. Von Schoultz continues:

One hour's cessation of hostilities was granted for burying our
dead, but having no shovels we could not do it — when the time was
out, the British steamers came down with heavy artillery, and the
battle began. As I could get no one to take the defence of the house
on our left flank, I went there myself with ten men. As I had
suspected, that house was most strenuously attacked. From the situation of the house I was not able to see how it went on in the other
houses and the mill. We must have been surrounded by at least two

thousand men, and a detachment of the eighty-third Regiment. My whole number of men, when this last battle began, was one hundred and eight ...

Among the wounded was Captain Wright, and he could see what was happening on the opposite shore:

During the engagement, I looked often toward the shores of Liberty and saw thousands thronging the beach at Ogdensburg, whose faint cheers reached us across the wave; and it embittered our hearts to know and feel that they whose tongues could beguile so successfully had not the moral courage to aid us in the hour of trial. We loaded our guns with pieces of broken iron, butts and screws, that we tore from the doors and fixtures of the mill.

But the action ended as it was bound to end. Nils von Schoultz concludes his report with these words:

I kept my position, though the roof crumbled to pieces over our heads by the British fire from their artillery, until dark, when I was informed that all had surrendered: I also then surrendered. I was stripped to the shirt sleeves by the militia, in the first heat of anger and fury. Even my bonnet was taken away. I lost my watch, trunk, money, and the clothing I had on.

In one of the many descriptions of this dramatic affair it is stated that the British force consisted of 5,000 men, two big gun-boats and seven small steamboats. The same writer – who signs himself simply Patriot – declares that the British had left 450 dead on the field of battle before they could force the patriots to surrender. His ardour for the cause led to a rather fanciful narrative of the final moments.

By midnight, everyone except our heroic leader had been captured. He alone maintained his station in the stone building, and kept up so uninterrupted a fire that the enemy believed the house to be full of patriots. At last they rushed in and he leaped down among them. Hurling themselves upon him like bloodhounds they tore off his clothes, they stole his hat and his watch. So ended the most remarkable conflict that has ever taken place on the soil of the North American continent.

According to another source, 'the gentleman, who was far too good for the company among whom he was seized, is said to have been deprived of a miniature of his wife . . .' an incident which added to the sufferings of his last days. Captain David Heustis, another of von Schoultz's men, wrote:

When it became known that Colonel von Schoultz was our leader, he was exposed to the vilest treatment. With his hands bound behind his back, mocked and derided, he was dragged to the boat at Prescott. When taken on board he was told by one of the officers that he was to be hanged at three o'clock next morning. Our hero replied calmly that he had often looked death in the eye before. Now he would try to take a little rest, as he had not had a wink of sleep for four nights. He sat down with his hands still bound, and fell asleep at once. On waking at four or five in the morning he remarked casually: 'They seem to have forgotten me. What next!' Later, on the way to Fort Henry, our brave leader was struck on the hip, and the wound never healed.

From Prescott the prisoners were dragged to Kingston, to be left at last in Fort Henry. 'They were tied in pairs with their hands bound behind their backs, and driven through the lighted streets of the town amid the yells and cheers of the mob, who pelted them with filth. The brave von Schoultz walked at their head – hatless!'

15

His Great Role

So this unhappy 'affair of the Windmill Point' ended in victory for the British, though with hundreds of killed and wounded. It had proved considerably more troublesome than was expected, admitted the Commander-in-Chief Sir George Arthur, in a report, although the number of dead, wounded and prisoners had been greatly exaggerated on both sides. Britain, her patience at an end, called the culprits to a merciless account. As the pitiable American government had no intention of preventing its citizens from disturbing the Queen's peace, it must take the consequences; and if the Americans fancied that they could 'bustle us out of Canada' they were very much mistaken. An end must now be made to the futile disturbances on the southern frontier.

The prisoners from Windmill Point were therefore brought to Kingston and to Fort Henry, that mighty stronghold defending Upper Canada. Lofty and menacing it stands on its headland, of which the base is swept by the waters of Lake Ontario as they rush down into the St Lawrence River. For tens of years men had laboured at its construction and reinforcement, and it now stood in its full majesty, surrounded by ditches and ramparts, by caponiers and jaunty Martello towers, and 'bristling with mounted cannons', but without ever having been threatened by an enemy or given the opportunity to display its strength. Rather the reverse, for only a few months before the clash at the Mill, in the spring of that same fateful year 1838, a small party of imprisoned rebels had succeeded in escaping from captivity in the fortress. There was in fact only one place in the innermost

part of it secure enough to hold the rebels – the filibusters –
who had been captured weapons in hand. To this day the guide
will not go past the cell where the victims of 1838 were in-
carcerated. These men are now called heroes of liberty, and
patriots: the name given them by their followers. To others
they were known as agitators, rebels and criminals.

It was clear to everyone that the fate of the prisoners was
sealed, and most people had to admit that a stern sentence was
justified; yet sympathy for them was deep and widespread. There
seemed something especially strange and poignant in the thought
that the unknown man who had fought oppression and tyranny
on the blood-soaked soil of Europe should have been overtaken
by Europe's vengeful powers on this side of the ocean. Some
may have felt pangs of conscience, and repented of the rumours
they had spread – idle stories that had lured their fellow-men to
destruction. Many tears were shed in secret over the stormy
petrel from abroad, and grief found expression in the supply of
clean linen and warm, home-knitted socks. Travellers to Kingston went via Prescott to behold the battlefield and to hear how
the 'invasion' had been met and repulsed.

One of these, Major J. Richardson, who was on his way from
Montreal to Toronto a day or so after the event, gives a circum-
stantial account of

... one of the best executed manoeuvres which took place during the
whole of the rebellion – namely, the passage of the St Lawrence, and
occupation of a strong position below Prescott, in Upper Canada, by
a numerous band of rebels and sympathizers, under the command of
the Pole von Schoultz. No spot could have been selected so well
adapted to the purpose, not of permanent defence, for that was never
contemplated, but of holding out until joined by the great body of
the population who, they had been led to believe, were ready to
flock to their standard the moment that a footing should be obtained.

He makes no mention of the talk in the officers' messes,
where the ability of the foreign leader was ungrudgingly acknow-

ledged, and reflections made upon the possibly disastrous results of the invasion, had the rebels adhered to the plan of attack on Prescott which von Schoultz was said to have proposed to the invisible commanders. But he continues:

Everything was tranquil in the neighbourhood of the late scene of contest, and but for the delapidation of the windmill, there was no evidence of its having been used for a military purpose – unless, indeed, I may except the appearance of a sentinel, one of a small militia piquet posted in the mill, who was pacing to and fro with an air of very justifiable importance, which seemed to announce to each passing stranger: 'Behold in me one of the captors of the redoubtable von Schoultz.' As for the windmill itself, it stood unharmed, and apparently as much undefaced by the shot which had been directed against it, as that which sustained the shock of the lance of the Knight of La Mancha. It struck me forcibly at the time that the selection of this position must have been the work of a soldier, who had well calculated his chances before moving in his game.

Major Richardson comments very frankly on the 'unparalleled military error' of Colonel Dundas of the 83rd, the officer in command of the British forces during those fateful ten days, and cannot understand why the men in the fort did not avail themselves of it to make their escape. He ends sourly:

Be this as it may, Colonel Dundas as senior officer, reaped the laurels, and Her Majesty honoured his victory with a companionship of the Bath.

On reaching Kingston, I found a court-martial already assembled for the trial of the prisoners, and composed of the principal militia-officers of the district. Their proceedings were summary, and conviction speedily followed – sentence of death having been passed on von Schoultz and several of his chief officers. I had a great curiosity to see the Pole who, with his fellow-prisoners, was confined in Fort Henry, then occupied by a detachment of the 93rd Highlanders. Availing myself, therefore, of an opportunity which presented itself, I mounted the tedious hill leading to the elevated and rather picturesque fortress, and soon found myself in the presence of him I sought.

I confess I was particularly and favourably impressed with the manner of this unfortunate man. No intimation whatever had been given to him of my intended visit, and yet when the bolt of the prison was withdrawn, and we suddenly appeared before him, his whole demeanour and attitude were such as could not fail to command respect. It being near the close of November it was of course cold; and around a stove of sheet iron, made intensely hot, were clustered a band of shivering wretches, one half of them without coats, and either warming their fingers or cooking some article of food – the whole exhibiting an appearance of despair and misery which left on the mind a sentiment of disgust.

But the relief to this picture was in the background. Beyond these squalid and contemptible looking beings, with folded arms and evidently acknowledging no moral assimilation, paced von Schoultz, with the dignified manner of one whose spirit not even in adversity, in her most hideous aspect, could bend into an association with vulgar minds. There was, moreover, a placidity and quiet resolution about his fine countenance that could not fail to interest, while the glance of a moment was sufficient to satisfy the beholder that, whatever his political faults – however misdirected his career of adventure – the man was a gentleman and a soldier. He was dressed rather neatly, wearing a dark frock coat, and a forage cap lightly and becomingly thrown over his brown hair, and his face, naturally pale, as much from the consciousness of the position in which he stood, as from the effects of his confinement, exhibited a mildness of expression which led me to wish that he had either died in the field or never entered it – at least with American sympathizers and Canadian *soidisant* patriots. Had this composed and half-melancholy air – this winningness of manner, been assumed for effect, it would of course have been estimated at its true value, but as I have before remarked, he knew not of the approach of any visitor, and not a minute had elapsed between the time the officer of the guard applied the key to the lock, and that to my introduction into the prison.

On seeing me, von Schoultz suddenly discontinued his meditative walk, and looked inquiringly, for my appearance had, as I soon after

learnt from his lips, impressed him with a belief that I was a countryman of his own, come to visit and console him in his hour of
extremity. I had on at the time a travelling dress consisting of a
Spanish zamara or fur jacket, with a velvet cap, tasselled, and hanging over the side of the head *à la Polonaise*, and these, with my
mustachios, certainly gave him every right to assume that I was a
foreigner. I went up to him, and accosting him in French, which
language he spoke very fluently, expressed my regret to see a person
of his appearance in such a situation – adding that I felt the more
surprise that a Pole, and in all probability a refugee who had often
shared her bounty, should, of all other people, have armed against
England – a country that had effected so much in amelioration of the
condition of his exiled countrymen. This seemed rather to startle
him, yet he replied that he had imagined he was rendering a service
to England, instead of injuring her, by adopting the course he had
pursued. He said that he had been fully given to understand, before
embarking in the expedition which had terminated so unfavourably
to him, that the whole of the Canadian people were anxious for
liberty and independence, and that he had fully expected, on landing
and gaining a temporary position, to be joined by armed thousands in
a few hours. This he concluded by asserting, had been the impression industriously circulated among those it was thought desirable
to attach to the ranks of the invaders, by certain secret committees
and lodges, which he declared existed everywhere throughout the
American Union (and particularly in the State of New York), to
an extent of which I could have no possible conception.

Richardson took this somewhat curious explanation for what
it was worth: a lame attempt to defend the indefensible; and
he did not pursue what he saw to be 'an unwelcome topic'. To
Richardson's inquiry as to whether he had ever been in Polish
service, von Schoultz replied

... that he had attained the rank of captain in the cavalry, and had
been engaged against Russia – that, like many others of his countrymen, he had been compelled to flee into exile, and was glad to
obtain service wherever it could be found. He added that he bitterly

regretted having embarked in the Canadian disturbances, into which he had been committed by false promises and falser hopes – that, however, he knew his fate, and was prepared to meet it.

During all this time von Schoultz spoke with a mildness of voice that was perfectly in harmony with the repose of his features, and when he remarked that, at my *premier abord,* he had been led to believe I was a countryman, he seemed to feel disappointment at his mistake. He, however, politely thanked me for having been interested enough in him to pay him a visit, and remarked, with a faint attempt at a smile, that it would soon be all over with him.

I could say nothing – I could offer him no word of hope or consolation, and I confess that I felt deeply pained, not more at the certainty of the fate that awaited him, but at the quiet and uncomplaining manner in which he resigned himself to that fate. I extended my hand, wishing him farewell. He grasped it energetically and for the first time betrayed anything like emotion. This, however, was subdued – so much so as to be almost imperceptible to anyone not closely watching the workings of his countenance. I withdrew to the door, where the two young officers of the 93rd (Lieutenants Hay and Studdert – the former a son of Sir Andrew Leith Hay, who introduced me), lingered spectators of the short scene, and as I once more turned, preparatory to leaving the place, I saw that von Schoultz had again resumed his limited walk. A moment after, and the heavy and creaking door had shut him from my view for ever.

The gloomy room in which the English major met von Schoultz and his poor, broken comrades-in-arms can hardly have been the cell in which the prisoner spent his last days. This is described as a 'cave, a small chamber in the heart of the mighty stone fortress, surrounded by massive walls and without any other light than the pale ray that fell through the thick iron grille of the ventilation hole. The entrance was barred by heavy oak doors with locks and iron bolts, reached only by a narrow, winding passage which had to be lit by a torch or lantern.' A space large enough for drama.

There are several consistent accounts describing the sequel.

Captain Heustis, who described the prisoner's departure from Prescott, continues:

The inquiry was nothing but a farce, for the gallant Pole was doomed in advance by those in power, and the court-martial had no more to do than pass sentence. All was done rapidly. The officers of the 83rd Regiment in particular, who had witnessed his heroism on the field of battle, sought his acquaintance and became deeply interested in his fate. They implored Sir George Arthur to spare his life, but that bloody tyrant turned a deaf ear to every supplication on behalf of the victim whom he had determined to destroy.

There is in existence a note written by Arthur on 6 November: 'I have considered the cases of the first three prisoners to be interrogated – Schoultz, Abbey and George – and have given the order for their execution. Awful work, but I believe it to be absolutely necessary.'

The British officers still tried to save him. They offered him as his defence counsel the promising young Macdonald, who is known to have been deeply moved by the fate of the prisoner. Creighton, his biographer, thinks that Macdonald might have seen 'the dark, exotic Pole' that wild Saturday night ten days earlier, when with proud indifference he paced ahead of the long, dismal line of prisoners through the garishly-lit streets of Kingston. At any rate Macdonald met him in the casemate which he shared with the 'two other officers of the brigand army, Abbey and George', These two were 'colourless, spiritless men, broken by their ill-fortune. Von Schoultz was of harder, purer metal, tempered in the flame of true revolution.' Creighton gives a detailed account of the trial.

On Wednesday 28 November the court-martial assembled. The long, low casemate with its bare, whitewashed walls was packed with officers of the Midland District Militia. They sat gravely and rigidly in their scarlet, silver-braided uniform jackets. Henry Draper, Solicitor-General to the District, put the case for the Crown. He was known as a skilful prosecutor, learned and cultivated, free from pettiness and harshness. He began by expounding the text of the law. His findings were that all the facts relating to the invasion were beyond dispute; that the prisoners were subjects of a friendly foreign power; that they had allied themselves with treacherous and rebellious British subjects; and that they had made war upon the Queen, wounding and killing a number of her subjects.

The first to be charged was Daniel George, an honest farmer from Onondaga County, and 'scarcely a heroic republican crusader'. He at once asked for an adjournment in order to prepare his defence.

The court passed to the next prisoner, 'General von Schoultz'. Draper repeated the charges and asked whether he pleaded guilty or not guilty. The accused stood up. 'His demeanour was perfect at this last, grotesquely tragic episode of his career,' says Creighton, and continues, 'He was a tall, handsome man, gentle-spoken and of aristocratic reserve. There was about him a romantic air of a foreign language, far countries and lost battles.'

The prisoner pleaded guilty. The president of the court-martial then reminded – indeed urged – the accused to put forward mitigating circumstances, whereby the sentence might be modified.

Now was the time for Macdonald to speak up. But he had no chance; no defence could be offered, for the prisoner repeated his plea of guilty. He admitted having been captured with weapons in his hands, but declared that he had taken up arms in the cause of freedom, adding bitterly that he now saw how disgracefully he and his companions in misfortune had been misled. Nevertheless he insisted that he was guilty, and did not want to be acquitted. He had settled his accounts with life. He accepted the death sentence as a just one – far more just than his judge could know. The true arbiter was his own conscience. He had heaped accusations upon himself and had tried in vain to stifle their murmurings. We must believe that Nils Gustaf no longer wished to live.

After sentence of death had been passed a despatch arrived from headquarters stating that as the prisoner held the rank of Field Marshal of Poland (!), he should not be executed in Kingston with the other condemned men, but in a fort. 'He was accordingly taken to Fort Henry and we never saw him again. The hour of parting, when he bade us farewell, filled every heart with sorrow. He said a kind word to each of us and admonished us all to die like men. His demeanour in this hour of bitter trial was what it had always been, manly and noble.' So Heustis concludes his account. His death sentence was read to him on 6 December. On the eighth he was executed.

From another source we learn that

When the hour for the execution arrived von Schoultz shook hands with those around him, and every eye was suffused with tears. He was prepared to die. . . . The Pole begged those Canadians who were friendly to him, and they were not few, to bury him just as he was and not to disturb his clothing . . . he betrayed no unmanly weakness; he marched with a firm and fearless step to the gallows, where his virtuous and patriotic life was brought to a premature close.

It is said that notwithstanding his request, the soldiers who buried him were driven by curiosity to open the breast of his coat, and there beheld, 'hung from a ribbon about his neck', the miniature of a very beautiful young girl. They quickly put the little portrait back in place and interred him with marks of honour. Clearly he had been afraid lest this treasure of his should be desecrated.

16

Verdict on a Hero

Is a man's fate less tragic for being shared by many? In reality, each man's end is unique, shaped by himself. This young man made his exit from life with unshaken dignity, almost with panache.

Simultaneously with von Schoultz, their commander, twelve rebels were sentenced and executed, of whom two blameless American citizens had been his closest colleagues. They too had been persuaded that they were joining this dangerous expedition in defence of liberty and to support their oppressed brothers. One of them, Abbey, wrote to his grown-up children that

> When our condition became hopeless, I could have taken opportunity to have made my escape across the line, but I could not bear the thoughts of deserting those brave, and many of them worthy and amiable young men to destruction; life, thus preserved, would not be worth possessing.

He also declares: 'Great delusion has, however, been entertained in relation to public opinion in Canada.' (It has indeed been stated, as Sir Arthur George wrote to Lord Fitzroy, that 'this invasion was in every sense American; only four Canadian refugees were involved'.) 'They are not prepared for republican institutions.'

Yet it was for 'the republican spirit' that honest Canadians and Americans were prepared to fight, and it was incomprehensible to these 'patriots' that Canada herself should send troops against them to help the British 'enemy' crush this spirit, which was to confer on Canada the same degree of freedom as the rest of the continent enjoyed.

Other American citizens were equally outraged by the events on their northern frontier:

When Texas rebelled against the government of Mexico, thousands of American citizens crossed the lines, and assisted in achieving independence. They went and returned as they pleased, without molestation from the government of the United States. Yet the contest in Texas was not so much a struggle for freedom as that in Canada.

States, in their dealings with one another, seldom put all their cards on the table, and though the rules of the game may be logical, they are seldom just and are difficult for the individual citizen to grasp. There is bitter truth in Captain Heustis's words:

Many are in the habit of looking at results instead of causes, and judging accordingly of the merit of a movement. If successful, the *rebel* becomes a *hero*; if unsuccessful, a *traitor.* . . . Had he [von Schoultz] fallen in battle we might have regretted his fate, without impugning its justice; but it will be a reproach to the British government, through all succeeding time, that this chivalrous champion of freedom was sacrificed, in the prime of life, for imitating the example of Lafayette and other heroes of the American revolution.

In the memoirs of Canadian 'patriots' von Schoultz is spoken of in high-flown terms. The sober chronicler has a poor opinion of him and his kind, but in the little towns along the Canadian border every local paper printed something about the brave foreigner. The following lines are typical:

Von Schoultz is esteemed by those who know him, as a gentleman, a man of science, a brave soldier and a true patriot. He engaged in this expedition, *because he was told that it was in the cause of liberty.* Some incidents are related by those who witnessed his conduct at the windmill and at Prescott, which prove him to have been a good engineer, a skilful commander, and a man of the most fearless intrepidity.

Whether it was this kind of commentary only which reached Thomas Phillips from America is not clear, but thanks to his unceasing efforts to discover the truth about this luckless man, Mary Campbell was at last sent a whole dossier containing exact information, extracts from court proceedings and quotations from letters and newspapers. It is hardly likely that Ann learned the whole truth at that time, but if she went through the documents later on, it must have been with mixed feelings. For what she read was a remarkable adventure story made up of a treacherous blend of fact and fiction.

Witnesses of the final act in the drama had been filled with admiration, and would hear nothing against von Schoultz. On 28 December 1838 there appeared in the *Syracuse Standard* a letter to the editor from a highly-respected citizen of Salina, a Mr Warren Green. This man we know to have been a liberal and to have opposed the increasingly dictatorial methods of the Church in purely lay matters. He is listed as No. 327 among The Brethren of Salina Lodge.

The editorial introduction to this letter runs as follows:

Colonel von Schoultz

Attempts have recently been made by the Tories of Canada, and their friends and coadjutors in the States, to produce the impression that this lamented martyr of liberty was a Russian emissary, sent to this country by the Emperor Nicholas to aid the rebellion in Canada. To rescue the name of von Schoultz from the disgrace and infamy which such a charge, if established, would bring upon it, we copy the following extract from a letter to the editor of the Syracuse Standard:

'Nils Gustaf Scholtewskii von Schoultz was of Swedish descent, a Pole by birth, and of noble extraction. He had just finished an education, which versed him deeply in the sciences, both useful and ornamental, and had acquired the highest literary honors of the principal and most celebrated Universities [*sic*] of Northern Europe, when he found himself engaged in that sanguinary and unequal contest between Poland and Russia, the unhappy termination of which lost to himself a country, and to that unfortunate country everything but a name. As he was ever extremely modest in his pretensions, I have seldom heard him revert to personal achievements incidental to events so memorable, and then only under circumstances of the highest excitement. But I have learnt from these occasional departures from self-reserve, incontestably from other sources, that the important part he enacted was brilliant with heroic adventures and hair-breadth escapes, the bare recital of which is calculated to enchain and captivate the most casual listener . . .

'In that sanguinary and decisive struggle before the walls of Warsaw, his father and a brother fell martyrs to the sacred cause of liberty [!]. His mother and a sister fled, in the disguise of peasants, but were taken and banished to Russia, and are now confined to a space of ten miles square of that Empire [!]. Himself gashed and scarred with wounds, but covered with imperishable glory – a fugitive wandering from country to country – friends and fortune lost, despoiled of home and kindred, with a constitution much impaired, he finally effected a landing on our shores, commonly denominated "the home of the brave and the land of the free".

'He evidently has been a traveller, as is to be inferred from his own declarations, as well as from rich stores of information he has acquired from actual observation. Sweden, Denmark, Finland, Lapland, Norway, Germany, Holland, Austria, Italy, Switzerland, France, Spain, Portugal, England, and finally America have been the theatre of his travels, and he had not only acquired a general geographic knowledge of them all but an intimate acquaintance with the habits, manners and customs of their inhabitants. I have heard him dwell long and eloquently on these, to me, novel and interesting topics – of Polar snows, and Italian skies, and of burning African suns – he had served beneath the scorching rays of the latter, and dwelt under the benign influence of the former – of Florence, its statuary, its picture galleries and, above all, of the urbanity and hospitality of its inhabitants. He spoke eight different dialects but,

at the time of his arrival here, he had only an imperfect knowledge
of our own.

'His contiguity to, and his father's interest in the celebrated mines
of Cracow [!], led him to an intimate knowledge of our principal
and staple article, salt. Thrown upon his own resources, in a land of
strangers, divested of every vestige of property but a few valuable
family relics, he cast about him with his usual energy for the means
of a livelihood, and these considerations brought him to the
Onondaga salines in the fall of 1836. Here he fitted up a small
laboratory – made his experiments – became confirmed in the truth of
his own theory, and succeeded in convincing at least one individual
of the practicability and utility of his improvement. In short, he
proceeded to Washington – obtained Letters Patent – visited and
analyzed the principal springs in Virginia – made the most favor-
able impressions wherever he extended his business or acquaintance,
and finally returned here according to promise, and put two of our
furnaces in operation on his plan *successfully*. While here, he listened
to the current report of Patriot suffering, of the oppressors and the
oppressed, of a vast population, seven-tenths of which waited the
coming of the liberators with open and extended arms. His sym-
pathizing soul was fired at the thought of again being permitted
to strike for freedom – his enthusiastic recklessness of danger led
him into its very vortex, and he has perished – ignominiously
perished.

'On a review of the sparkling incidents of his brief and romantic
career, I still think on him as the creature of a high wrought fancy
rather than of sober reality – like a meteor of uncommon brilliancy,
which has suddenly illumined the path of my dull existence, and as
suddenly disappeared for ever.

Warren Green.

Salina, 28 December, 1838.'

We can only suppose that this fable had been inspired by its
hero, and perhaps too by his fellow-combatants from Poland.
The truth, though different, would have been no less dramatic.

In the mixed chorus of panegyric and abuse, one voice rings
out more soberly and with greater veracity than the rest. In the

Commercial Adviser – neither date nor place is given, though the origin was most likely New York – the following appeared:

An account has been given us by a gentleman who expresses great confidence in its truth, of the life of Colonel von Schoultz, which differs from any that state him to be a Pole. According to his information, Colonel von Schoultz was a native of Sweden, the nephew to the Governor of Swedish Finland [*sic*]. He served in the Polish revolutionary army, and afterwards with the French in Algiers. He is said to have married, at Florence, the daughter of Colonel Campbell of the East India Company's service, and we are assured that ladies of this city, one of whom is named to us, were on terms of intimacy with his wife, and were present at his marriage. For some unknown reason he left his wife at Cronstadt [*sic*] and emigrated to this country; was for some time in the city of New York, and then removed to Salina where he discovered the process mentioned by the Onondaga paper, and was believed to have realized a considerable sum of money.

What could induce him to engage in the foolish and criminal expedition that cost him his life, is a mystery to those who knew him here; but the secret is to be found probably in a roving and unsettled disposition, a Quixotic passion for adventure, and that ardent love for liberty which led him to take up arms in Poland. He was a man of excellent education, of almost universal knowledge, of polished manners, and in conversation fluent and interesting.

17

Everyday Heroine

WHILE Nils, pursued by the Furies, rushed upon his fate, Ann was living in the timelessness of anxiety and distress; for having received no letters from him after the two from Baltimore she must have realized at last that she had been betrayed and deserted. Then, one after another during the early spring of 1839, the last terrible reports came in. At first she found a faint ray of hope in the reiterated statement that the man Scholtewskii von Schoultz was a Pole. It was just possible that this N. S. von Schoultz had been a distant and hitherto unknown relative. But very soon all doubts were dispelled.

When Ann wrote to friends in New York, asking them to tell her all they knew and could discover about the tragedy, she received an immediate reply: no talk now of letters lost in the post! Dated 13 July 1839 and signed M.B. – Mary Bell, one of Ann's faithful friends from the days in Florence – the answer to Ann's 'sweet, sad letter' of April is tender, tactful and sincere:

... heart-rending as the task is to me, I will undertake it, for I love you too well to refuse you anything. As soon as I read the account in the newspaper, and saw the name (altho' disguised and passing for a Pole) I felt convinced in my own mind that it was *him* I had always hoped to meet again and in order to ascertain some particulars I wrote imm: to Warren Green Esq of Salina who you may have seen was mentioned as his Executor. I wrote as delicately as possible in the hope still of finding that the unfortunate subject of our correspondence might be a stranger to me. His reply was prompt and explicit but left me still in error by stating that the Mr V. S. he knew and who had been an inmate in his house represented himself to be a *Pole* and had often mentioned having a cousin in this country who bore 'exactly his name'!!! and that since his imprisonment at Fort Henry had again alluded (in a letter to him) to *that cousin.*

This, for a time, held out a ray of hope which was again extinguished by various reports of his having been in this city stirring up it was said the numerous Poles here to go to Canada, and the description I had of his person left me but little to doubt. As I understood that Warren Green had administered to his estate and took the deepest interest in his fate I wrote again and the second letter totally removed all doubts as to his identity! The letter was sealed with the *seal of the family you use* and the copy of his signature was the facsimile of your husband's!!

She goes on to give the contents of Nils's will, quoting verbatim from Warren Green's letter:

[After certain bequests] 'He then directs me to divide the balance into 4 equal parts – one of the parts he wills – these are the exact words – To Mistress Anna von Schoultz daughter of the late Alexander Campbell of Calcutta or in case of her death to her next heir. . . . One part to Mistress Joanna von Schoultz widow of the late Vice-Governor Nils Frederic v. Schoultz and daughter of the late General Gripenberg of Finland, and the remaining 2 parts to myself and 2 other individuals of my family.'

The press of course had more to say. Of the amount

about £4000 – one quarter is bequeathed to the girl he was to have married, £100 to the Catholic College at Kingston, and £400 to the widows and orphans of the British militia who fell at Johnstown. This last is an act of contrition which exhibits an uncommon mind, and causes one to regret that such a man should have engaged in such a cause.

So the principal features of the Mill Point drama were brought to light, and reached first London and then Mary Campbell during the spring and early summer of 1839. How much she imparted to her daughter is uncertain; did Ann ever hear about the girl in Salina?

Not a line from Nils Gustaf's own family has been found. Ann never mentions them in this connection, and seldom at any time. Aunt Ulrique, on the other hand, was a steadfast – if not always easy – friend to her and hers.

Letters to Ann from the relatives in England go into no details. They are deeply sympathetic, tactfully encouraging and full of praise for her behaviour.

Ann was so stricken that she bowed almost meekly under the blow. Among the fragments of her journal we find one page, perhaps part of a prayer:

I shall have nothing with which to reproach thee. Thou hast been the means appointed by God's good wisdom from all time to bring me through suffering, I hope nearer to Him. O Thou Almighty, grant indeed that this great sorrow may be to the purifying of my soul, that I may not harden myself under the mighty hand that chasteneth me, so as to require more and severer punishment. Oh may it fully work out in me the purpose for which it was sent – putting away all earthly hopes, and desires, and supports, I may look alone to Thee for my sufficient and abiding portion.

On another scrap of paper that has been preserved she wrote down her resolve for the future:

Now I will strive but to think of him but as one whom I much loved, who was led away from me for a season, but who has now entered into the Rest of the weary, one who suffered for all he had sinned, one whom, I doubt it not, the God who had gifted him with many such rare gifts accepted even at the eleventh hour, and brought his heart back to Him, purified and made holy, when all the delusions of passion, and mist of vain hopes and desires, has passed away – and thus in another world, when I meet thee again . . .

Yet as time went on, anger and bitterness welled up. She took down the portrait that hung over little Tuttan's bed, unable to endure the child's continual questioning: 'When's Daddy coming home?' Later, when she dared to look again at the like-ness, she marvelled wrathfully that she had ever read tenderness or nobility in that arrogant, false face. She destroyed the portrait. It has been said that Ann never knew how her husband died. 'Executed' was Mary Campbell's reply to her daughter's frantic questioning. For months their conversation turned upon a single theme: how could Nils have deserted those to whom he had vowed his life-long love? How could such a thing come about? What happened to him? What did anyone know of Nils's life in America? After one of these futile discussions Mama declared that the subject must never be mentioned again; and from that time onwards Ann never refers to it. Not even to her daughters did she speak of Nils's end, or pronounce his name. After her death a sealed envelope was found, containing letters and docu-ments in which Nils von Schoultz is mentioned. Her journals she censored the year before her own death; she was then not quite fifty, yet she was an old woman. When Nils Gustaf left her she was twenty-two; at twenty-five she was a widow.

The outline of her life after Nils Gustaf's death is soon traced. It appears that the hitherto so dependent, helpless, spoilt young woman stepped resolutely out of her vague, unfulfilled dreams of bliss, to take over the management of her family. As early as the autumn of 1836, when she went to Vörta, she wrote in practical terms to her mother about deliveries and prices, grinding, and deliveries of whole grain. The most re-markable feature of this period is that she was no longer relying wholly on her mother's judgement in their confused business affairs: 'I hope you have not yet replied to Uncle's letter regard-ing these matters, as I would like to see your letter, Mama, please.'

From the beginning, Ann von Schoultz had conceived a resigned contempt for Karlskrona. On first driving in over the long bridge she had seen nothing of the friendly, gaily-painted rows of houses gleaming through the summer twilight. She may not have had time either to notice the snug little cabins perched up the sea cliffs, before complaining that nobody could possibly walk on the horrible cobblestones of those broad, empty streets. She seems secretly to have shared the opinion of Nauckhoff, that sour provincial governor, who said that Karlskrona was a dreary town where people lived on codfish and gossip. And soon enough she could smell the gossip sneaking round the corners of the Superintendent's house, whispering at the back door and smirking in at tea-time.

She made one attempt to move to Vörta. But, just as Colonel de Frese had predicted, the mill ground anything but gold, and the dwelling-house there was delapidated and chilly.

When all seemed lost, the tide turned. Baron Casper Wrede offered the English ladies a refuge in his newly-acquired property Djupadal: a delightful place not far from Karlskrona. Casper Wrede was the brother of Agathe Wachtmeister and, since her widowhood, steward of the Wachtmeister estates. He lived in one wing of Johannishus.

After this move into the country, life began to regain something of its old peace and contentment. Day followed day, one much like another, and season melted into season without dramatic contrasts. The rich landscape was marvellously colourful: brown, bursting leaf-buds in the blue air of spring; soughing canopies of oak and beech; golden fields of corn; the grey of autumn over wet roads and stony slopes; and the mild mists and snow of winter.

But outside time, beyond day and night, sounded the voice of the falls: the rush and thunder of Djupafors in Ronneby river which swept past Djupadal on its way to the sea. With the changing winds its voice came now soft as a whisper, now loud and majestic, yet always it brought consolation and serenity to Ann. To Mary Campbell the sound came like a greeting from the waters of Scotland.

Here Ann could feel at home. She was freed from the kindly

importunities of people for whom she cared nothing. There was soft earth beneath her feet and she could walk for miles with her active little daughters. Her children were with her constantly: 'they are my life and my only happiness', she wrote over and over again. She regarded their upbringing as her chief duty; but there was time for much else in that tranquil place. Her mother persuaded her to take down her guitar from the wall, and to carry her sketch-book with her on her walks. She wrote letters, of course, and read a great deal of both old and new works. Among the new ones were Fredrika Bremer's books which soon found their way to Karlskrona. Countess Wachtmeister and Casper Wrede were Fredrika's cousins, and through them Ann received the new publications early. She was at once charmed by their freshness and spirit of rebellion, and courageously translated *The President's Daughters* and *Home,* and later *Nina,* though she earned no money by this work until Mrs Howitt took her under her wing.

Ann struggled earnestly and humbly with her own education and development. As it was natural that the local pastor and itinerant preachers should visit 'the ladies at the Manor', we may assume that her acquaintance with Pastor Stéenhoff, the great temperance champion, was formed through one or other of them. At one time his name is often mentioned in the journal, and a letter from a gossipy friend declares that he was in hopes of making a match of it with 'a rich foreign lady'.

True friends in Karlskrona did not forget Ann and her family in their solitude; on the contrary, they were faithful and very kind. They obtained books for her from the library and Höök's bookshop. Captain Byström, who was the soul of all that could be called culture in Karlskrona sent sheet-music to Djupadal, and Fru Arnoldson, whose fine singing could fill a whole evening with enchantment, sent 'the most amiable invitation' to her musical soirée. Ann went to it, and to 'a great supper-party at the Malmborgs' '.

Many names of people in the Karlskrona of those days appear in Ann's journal, which she had taken up again: among them that of Countess Puke and her daughters, who drove up to her door in a carriage and four. Dear old Chamberlain Lagerbielke came to Vörta in person to fetch his sacks of flour. But when Countess Frédérique Ruuth sent repeated invitations to Ann and her little girls, Ann noted curtly: 'Now it is too late.' But nothing was more delightful – or more sorrowful – than when gentle Countess Wachtmeister showed pictures from her long sojourn in Italy. Tears flowed with the memories of what had been.

Dearest to Ann of all her friends were Casper and Hedda Wrede. After the wedding in June 1837 these most likeable young people settled for a short time into a wing of Johannishus, before moving to Djupadal, which may have had to be furbished up a little for the young baroness. For a month or so after they had moved into this permanent home, they allowed the Scottish ladies to stay on, on the ground floor. They all met daily and hourly, and never a cloud dimmed their friendship. Less often, but just as gladly, they continued to visit each other after Ann and her family moved to Johannishus.

Ann found another good and reliable friend in Major Adolf Palander: a wise counsellor and tireless assistant throughout all her years in Sweden. What did he not do for young Fru von Schoultz! As late as the year 1840 he induced master-tailor Nordfelt of Stockholm to make a substantial discount on a bill which the Lieutenants von Schoultz had forgotten to pay. The mother of these young men had brushed the matter aside, recommending the tailor to claim his few hundred crowns from Nils Gustaf's rich widow. In time, Major Palander sorted out other more mysterious debts, and when they were all receipted to the last penny, Ann left the country in which she had tasted what crumb of happiness fate had allowed her, and where she had suffered the bitter sorrow of the deserted and bereft.

Mary Campbell had stood steadfastly at her daughter's side. Did she feel to blame for what had happened to Ann? We know nothing of this, nor of Ann's thoughts on the matter. Neither in letters nor journals do we find a hint of reproach; only love, gratitude and obedience.

Together with her mother and her little daughters, Ann moved to Heidelberg in 1842 and, after Mary Campbell's death in 1843, to Darmstadt.

By then her sister Mary had left them. During the years in Sweden that attractive feather-brain had grown up, made many friends in Karlskrona and was present at all the grander social events. Once, on the occasion of a royal visit, she was chosen to present the customary bouquet. ('Why she, of all people?' demanded Aunt Elisabeth.) But she could not endure the disaster that had overtaken the family. She regarded it as a crushing misfortune which fell most unjustly upon herself, and threatened to ruin her whole life. She sat like an imprisoned princess in a wretched wooden castle, without any hope of being discovered by a prince of Albion. But the well-known, almost classic escape-route for a daughter of Britain was open to young Mary: she would sail for India.

She wept and threatened to die on Mama's hands if she could not leave this detestable existence, this dismal climate, this country which meant nothing to her. . . . So, suitably equipped, and after a breathing-space in London with Aunt Elisabeth and kind old Uncle Thomas, she set forth – as her mother had done before her – across the wide seas to India, where she indeed soon found safe harbour. She married a distant relative – most suitable – Colonel Simon Frazer Hannay, and lived there, it was said, as gaily as in her youth.

Nils Gustaf had gone; nevertheless it was he who in the end made the great decisions in Ann's life. His little daughters were not allowed to forget their father's Swedish language – Ann saw to that – and although the girls always spoke to each other in

English, and went on year-long visits to foreign parts, their Swedish remained pure, and rich in vocabulary. When the time came for Florence and Anna to be confirmed, their mother took them 'home' to Ronneby, in Sweden.

The relatives in Finland had soon learnt of the fate of their unstable kinsman, and Cousin Constantin Nils Lorentz wrote to Ann, begging her to 'return to the family home in Finland'. He added: 'The crime of a Schoultz must be atoned for by a Schoultz.'

Ann hesitated, but the exchange of letters led at last to a blissful summer visit to various relatives in Finland, to be followed later by a stay of more than a year in a home of her own in Helsinki. In the course of that year, Ann saw both her daughters married.

Gentle little Anna's wedding to Admiral Hampus Furuhjelm was a society sensation, and her life-story has been preserved for posterity in the charming book written by her daughter Annie Furuhjelm, *People and Their Lives*. Six months later Florence married her second cousin Carl Fredrik Sebastian von Schoultz – much against his mother's will – and enjoyed a life with him full of interest, variety and love.

Ann herself never emerged from the shadow cast by the name of Nils Gustaf, yet she gave her daughters no cause to do more than guess at the chill of that shadow.

He was just not there, and 'one doesn't ask about things like that.'

18

After a Century of Silence

'Dear, beauteous death, the jewel of the just . . .'
Henry Vaughan.

INDEED, a hundred years and more went by before anyone
dared to ask questions. Or, if they did, the family refused to
answer them. Nils Gustaf's name was never mentioned. Silence
reigned.

However, his later descendants felt less stricken and less outraged than his wife. They had not her reason for regarding his
harebrained escapade in Canada against 'the Queen's peace' as
high treason against the beloved mother country. Secretly they
felt some sympathy with the ever turbulent blood of their race;
not from a wish to excuse, but rather to render a measure of
justice to the condemned man.

The Victorian idyll, so deeply shaken by the sins of a poor
lieutenant, has long since been swept by greater storms than the
Upper Canadian Rebellion, and rootless people are sucked into
storm-centres now as then. Foolish rumours of oppression are
readily believed, arouse sympathy, attract 'helpers' and trigger
off disasters. To this day conspirators with the sincerest motives
are at work on foreign soil in the name of freedom.

Today too, there are emigrés in every quarter of the world,
every other one of them with a *ci-devant* air about him, and
most of them have of course lost millions – 'as is known from a
reliable source'. Compared with these, a Polish marshal's baton
and a provincial governor's seat in the Finland of the Swedish

era are minor myths, while penniless younger sons are still to be met with.

Nils Gustaf's passion for freedom is something we can believe in. Did not the students in Finland and Sweden drink toasts to the Pole? The wounded prisoners from the Finnish regiments who were tended by Swedish doctors in Warsaw had been persuaded that they were helping the Poles against the French; that they were fighting Napoleon's compatriots who had sold Finland to the Russians! All depends on how the facts are presented.

But can there be any defence of the man's betrayal of his young wife? Was Nils Gustaf just a charming scoundrel who knew that one fine day he would be moving on? Did he feel no remorse for the hearts he broke? He had doubted his own fidelity during the very first months of being in love, even if the will to it was there.

Nils Gustaf had been brought up among boys and chosen a life among hard-living men. He had been introduced early to the world of great ideas, and great ideas are seldom to be restrained by obligations towards mere people. When the liberator from Poland had singed his wings in Algeria, Florence came like an intoxicating, rosy dream, and he was swept off his feet. Yet if he alone had borne the responsibility for his trusting young wife he might not have deserted her. He might have carried her with him in his pursuit of fortune. She might have starved and wept, but she would have kept his dour love, and borne it as well as she bore her bitter loneliness. He could not write to her on the last night of his life, and no explanations then would have made her relent. Yet it may have been her portrait – the miniature painted in Florence – that hung next to his heart when he mounted the scaffold.

What came to the doomed man with the wind that blew over Old Fort Henry? Kindly memories? Memories of a happy little boy with his toboggan in the sparkling snow below his grandmother's manor house ... a slim young subaltern among the prince's guests in the palace of Stockholm ... moonlit nights on Ponte Vecchio ... mild autumn days in an old garden in Karlskrona ... Auld Lang Syne? Or did grimmer recollections of high stakes, of gold lost and won, rush upon his mind? Dishonour ... blood of the innocent ... homelessness, continual departure. Or was he thinking of a pretty girl in Salina and the soft arms that tried to hold him back?

At that moment the past may have seemed to him meaningless and petty, repented of, erased by pain. All that remained of his dreams of achievement and greatness was the ignominy he had brought upon himself; yet he could welcome death now that he had been granted those last sublime days. As Karen Blixen writes: 'As the good citizen finds happiness in the fulfilment of his duty to society, the proud man finds his in the accomplishment of his destiny.'

Nils Gustaf Scholtewskii von Schoultz accomplished his destiny on a splendid stage. Canada's proudest fortress served as his footstool; below its mighty walls rolled the waters of the St Lawrence; above him the vast vault of the sky, and all about him darkness and silence.

There he bade farewell to life.

Epilogue: The Canadian Troubles 1837–8

THOSE who had inspired and supported the attack on the Windmill at Prescott, Upper Canada, were outraged at the severity of the sentences passed on the leaders of the expedition and the swiftness with which they were carried out. Yet even as the trials proceeded another invasion of Upper Canada was taking place. In the early morning of 3 December 1838 a force of one hundred and fifty men crossed the river from Detroit in a commandeered steamer and attacked the town of Windsor. The officer commanding the expedition, 'General' Bierce, proclaimed liberty for the oppressed Canadians, then beat a hasty retreat, leaving his senior field commanders to be killed in battle by the local militia and a number of their men to be captured. During the 'battle', which lasted an hour or two, the Patriots were supported by the cheers of thousands from the Detroit shore, as Nils von Schoultz had been by the ineffective crowds on the waterfront at Ogdensburg, New York.

It is easy to feel now that the Canadian authorities were unduly alarmed and severe. The so-called Patriot Wars were little more than a series of bloody scuffles chiefly notable for their brutality. But the Hunters' Lodges were believed to have enrolled more than 150,000 members from Vermont to Michigan, sworn to promote liberty starting with Canada. Their ardour had been sharpened by a promise of 300 acres per man of good Canadian land. No nation could be casual about such a menace on its borders, even in times of prosperity and contentment. And Upper Canada in 1838 was neither prosperous nor content.

There had been rebellions in both Upper and Lower Canada in December 1837, the final flame-up of long smouldering discontent. Though basically different in their origins and deficient in revolutionary passion, both had aimed at reducing the power of an executive appointed by their British Lieutenant Governors. Badly managed as the uprisings were, they achieved enough co-ordination of timing to keep the limited defence forces at full stretch, and had there been a general will to radical change they could hardly have been contained.

Lower Canada (now Quebec) had begun to recover from the trauma of the 1759 conquest on the Plains of Abraham only to find its French speaking majority dominated by alien governors and exploited by an Anglo-American mercantile class. Control of the elected assembly did not mean effective control of its own affairs. Though the British-appointed Governor, the judges and the law officers were not wholly sympathetic with the mercantile group, the latter commanded substantial influence and could press its interests in the language of the Executive Council.

Petty frustrations and minor tyrannies had accumulated into major grievances, and rising arguments had led to threats of violence. The lines in Lower Canada were drawn roughly between French- and English-speaking, between Catholic and Protestant – and the battalions, though not big, were on the side of the English. The non-military on both sides began to arm and to drill, and fights that became riots occurred with increasing frequency.

As the clouds darkened the few British regiments had been sent to Lower Canada. When rebellion broke out in December 1837 the badly led and badly organized patriots were quickly and brutally crushed. A few of the insurgents were executed and a few exiled; the leaders escaped to the United States.

The rebellion in Upper Canada (now southern Ontario) had no racial overtone. The province, which was English-speaking, had as its core a population made up of Loyalist or Tory refugees from the American war of Independence and of Americans who had subsequently emigrated, attracted by the promise of good land. To these, in the years following the Napoleonic wars, had been added a substantial number of English, Irish and Scots immigrants, many of them already blown upon by the rising winds of reform.

The troubles of Upper Canada were probably growing pains rather than symptoms of any deep-seated malaise. The opening-up of the country had not kept pace with the flow of immigration. Government was in the hands of a mildly repressive establishment, more comfortable and arrogant than corrupt, slow to change and profoundly distrustful of democracy. Calls for reform met stiffening resistance, and things came to a head when the reformers, led by William Lyon Mackenzie, elected a majority in the Assembly in 1834, only to find their triumph comparatively meaningless.

Wise management and a will to accommodation could still have avoided an outbreak. But the newly appointed Lieutenant Governor, Sir Francis Bond Head, was over-confident and hasty when only good sense and calm could help. It was a jest of fate that set the rash, clever and ultimately silly Bond Head against the peevish crusading fervour of William Lyon Mackenzie. The aim of the Reformers was constitutional reform – vaguely defined as responsible government. When that appeared to be denied, Mackenzie called for republicanism and union with the United States. This alienated many of his supporters and committed him to desperate courses.

Rebellion when it came on 7 December 1837 was virtually finished in a single 'battle' north of Toronto. The discontented were numerous but they were widely dispersed and wretchedly armed. Hopeless communications added to a sketchy organization and a lack of skilled leaders delivered the rebels into the hands of the only slightly less inept government forces. Less than five hundred of the many thousand reformers were present when battle was joined at Montgomery's Tavern; and half of them were armed only with pikes and cudgels.

The British regulars had all been sent out of Upper Canada to confront greater dangers near Montreal. The defence of Toronto rested with a motley collection of about a thousand volunteer militia, but possessing some light artillery and resolutely led. The battle was over in a few minutes and many contingents of men tramping in to join Mackenzie arrived to find him gone, and quickly changed their allegiance.

The little explosion let much of the heat out of the rebellion movement. Loyal volunteers by the thousands poured into Toronto or moved into the more disturbed areas, hunting rebels. Two ringleaders were put on trial and later hanged. The majority were not to be found. Many were already across the American border and the rest in hiding. Within two or three weeks the province was outwardly tranquil and aggressively loyal.

The years of mounting unrest had not attracted great attention in the United States though as events moved toward a crisis there had been meetings of sympathizers in some of the border cities. Times were bad on both sides of the frontier and in addition to genuine sympathizers there were large numbers of unemployed and of the drifters to be found in all ports, ready for any agitation. Since Lower and Upper Canada lay along the St Lawrence River, Lake Ontario and Lake Erie, the refugees from the abortive rebellions made their escapes into New York, Ohio and Michigan. The story told there of great wrongs and oppression at the hands of British governors, and of a people waiting to be liberated, was only too easy for Americans to believe. At this early moment of the American dream it could produce only one response.

William Lyon Mackenzie, after an exciting escape from Upper Canada, was given a hero's welcome in Buffalo. Within a few days he had established the Provisional Government of Upper Canada on Navy Island in the Niagara River and issued scrip for the purchase of supplies and arms for an invasion of Canada. Volunteers were each to have 300 acres of Crown land. Arms, including cannon, found their way to Navy Island apparently from the arsenals of Buffalo and food was either purchased with scrip or supplied by the donations of sympathizers. A fife and drum band marched in the streets of Buffalo carrying the new flag of Upper Canada and recruiting for the invasion. Speeches were made about the Spirit of '76 and the Spirit of '37. Mackenzie appointed an American, 'General' Van Renselaer, as his military commander, though in time it appeared that the general had nothing to recommend him but a distinguished name.

For two to three weeks the little army of perhaps two or three hundred Canadian refugees and American liberators lived in squalid misery in the Niagara River daily bombarding the Canadian shore. Opposite them at Chippewa a strong force of militia patrolled the river bank day and night. The force on Navy Island had been supplied by scow from Buffalo but in late December a steamer destined to be famous was acquired for the ferrying of men and supplies. The steamer was named the *Caroline*.

Up to this point the force on the Canadian shore had not fired on Navy Island for fear of a breach of neutrality. In the face of Mackenzie's cannonade they had stood on the defensive but the time had come to act. On the night of 28 December 1837 a small boat party put out from the Canadian shore in search of the *Caroline*. Expecting to find her moored at Navy Island they saw her instead tied up at Fort Schlosser on the American shore and went straight on. She was quickly and boldly boarded and though a fight developed she was captured and towed out into the stream and set on fire. Above the falls the blazing steamer stranded on a rock and burned to the water-line while the boat party slipped away in the darkness.

The *Caroline* incident changed the whole focus of border

excitement. At least one man, an American citizen, had been killed in the boarding and others were wounded. Rumour described the action as a massacre and pictures of the blazing vessel hurtling over Niagara Falls were circulated. Sympathy for oppressed Canadians became active demands for war with Britain and the liberation and acquisition of Canada. Up to this point the government of President Jackson had been firmly if ineffectively neutral but the burning of the *Caroline* made the president's position even more difficult – whether it changed his attitude or not. In the Patriot movement that now developed rapidly all along the border, to erupt in a series of piratical adventures, the rallying cry became: 'Remember the *Caroline*.'

In Washington it was at least recognized that the *Caroline* incident was the inevitable reply to flagrant breaches of the neutrality laws. If control was not established there would be more, and the demand for war must become general, and irresistible. General Winfield Scott on the New York border and General Brady at Detroit were given strict instructions to enforce neutral behaviour. But their resources were inadequate to smother such a fire and Governors Marcy and Mason were looking the other way.

All through the spring and summer of 1838 the growth of the Hunters' Lodges linked to the Patriot exiles went on. Undoubtedly their numbers included many sincere idealists who believed the Canadians wanted liberty and must be helped to secure it. Some good men were to die for their misreading of the confusing evidence and some, like Nils von Schoultz, would be dragged down by the lunatic fringe. For the good men were far outnumbered by the emotional and misled boys, and by the hard cases who cried liberty but meant plunder. The stages by which Nils von Schoultz became involved in the expedition against Prescott will probably remain obscure. Such a romantic could hardly have escaped the excitement that swept the south shore of Lake Ontario from Niagara to Ogdensburg throughout 1838. Once involved he became the prisoner of his capacity and probably of his pride. His experience placed him among the leaders and when others backed out or fumbled von Schoultz went on. In all the circumstances he followed a forlorn hope but, unsupported, he found a defensible position and held it resolutely, yielding only when he was overwhelmed. His inexperienced men fought as men fight only when they are well led. And when it was over von Schoultz faced the consequences with a dignity and bravery that almost gave nobility to the foolish adventure.

The Thousand Islands in the St Lawrence became a pirate's nest during that spring and a passenger steamer, the *Sir Robert Peel*, was seized and burned by William Johnson and his gang, later to behave ingloriously at the Battle of the Windmill. There were Patriot raids from the vicinity of Plattsburg, from Niagara, across Lake Erie and two or three in the Detroit area. For a year the border was virtually beyond control until the Battles of the Windmill and Windsor with their stern aftermaths. With the hanging of the ringleaders that followed these two battles, the transportation of some to Van Diemen's land and the deportation of the misguided boys to the United States, the border was tranquillized. In the months that followed the Hunters made speeches with diminishing fervour, drank toasts to fallen comrades and gradually faded from view.

Many of the Hunters' speeches took the line that the Canadians were cowardly and unworthy of liberty, though to begin with they had decided that the Canadians were to have liberty even if it killed them. But if they had cared to inquire or to listen they would have known that the Canadians wanted and needed reform, given that they would have all the liberty they wanted. What they didn't seek was the kind of liberty so recently thrust on Texas.

What the Hunters could also have known and ultimately did realize was that their fiercest foes were not British regular soldiers but the Canadian militia. They could have known that the shores of the St Lawrence and Lake Ontario had been settled by the disbanded Loyalist regiments from the War of Independence: The King's Royal Regiment of New York, the Royal Highland Emigrants, Jessup's Rangers, Roger's Rangers, Butler's Rangers.

Reform came to Canada thanks to a radical British peer, Lord Durham, sent out to investigate the rebellions. His report was to result in the responsible government that became the keystone of the future British Commonwealth. A less happy outcome was a deep lingering distrust of American intentions, pervasive in Canada but strongest in Ontario.

Almost thirty years later John A. Macdonald, the lawyer who defended von Schoultz, was Prime Minister of Canada (at that point Ontario and Quebec). In 1866 he was struggling with his colleagues to work out an acceptable confederation of the parts of what is now Canada. The difficulties seemed almost insurmountable until once again invasion from the United States simplified the issues. A force of disbanded Irish veterans of the Northern Army, members of the Sinn Fein (or the Fenian movement), chose this moment for the liberation of Canada from British tyranny. They were easily beaten back but they had confirmed Macdonald's long memory from the Patriot Wars and swept away regional objections to Confederation.

JOHN MORGAN GRAY

Sources and Bibliography

Long though this list is, it remains incomplete. The material has been collected over a long period – between twenty and thirty years – with the sole object of completing the von Schoultz archives in *Riddarhuset* (the Hall of Knights) in Finland. Much of it has proved impossible to verify. Documents and manuscripts in the family archives relating to Nils Gustaf von Schoultz:

Nils Gustaf von Schoultz: letters
Ann Campbell von Schoultz: letters and journals
Carl von Schoultz: Memoirs
Nils Fredrik von Schoultz: *Anteckningar om vår släkt,* and *Egna lefnadsöden*
Elizabeth Phillips: letters
Mary Phillips: letters

For records of earlier generations, and of childhood and schooldays, I am indebted to:

Andersson, Otto: *Johanna von Schoultz. I sol och skugga* (Åbo, 1939)
Gripenberg, G. A.: *Generalmajor Hans Henrik Gripenberg* (Helsingfors, 1957)
Jutikkala, Eino: *Sääksmäen pitäjän historia* (Helsinki, 1934)
Kuujo, E. O.: *Piirteitä Gripenbergin internaattikoulusta 1812–1822* (Hist. Arkisto 55, Helsinki, 1955)
Nervander, E.: *Strödda uppsatser* (Helsingfors, 1911)

Information regarding N. G. von Schoultz's military training has been taken from:

Anteckningar om Svea Artilleriregemente 1794–1894 (Stockholm, 1898)

The section on Poland is based on:

Backman, Ch. Pierre: *Sverige och Polen* (Göteborgs Handels- och Sjöfartstidning, 1930)

Stille, J. S.: *Anteckningar under en resa till och från Warschau vid slutet af Polska Frihets-Kriget 1831* (Lund, 1834)

The chapters on Florence, the journey north, Karlskrona, Edinburgh and London are based exclusively on letters and journals in the family archives. Additional information relating to Ann von Schoultz's sojourn in Blekinge has been taken from:

Bromé, J.: *Karlskrona stads historia* (1930–34)

Feuk, L.: *Historiska skizzer och silhouetter* (Christianstad, 1883)

Föreningen Gamla Karlskrona: Year Books

Gamla svenska städer (Stockholm, 1915–26)

N.G. von Schoultz's stay in America is mentioned in countless printed and unprinted documents, many of them contradictory. To a large extent they may be traced to identical sources, however varied the opinions expressed in them. Here are some:

The Arthur Papers, edited by C. R. Sanderson (Toronto, 1943)

Beauchamp, the Rev. William M.: *Past and Present of Syracuse* and *Onondaga County* (1908)

Belleville Intelligence (1838)

Bourinot, J. C.: *Canada under British Rule 1760–1900* (Cambridge, 1900)

Carmer, C.: *Dark Trees to the Wind* (New York, 1949)

Coburgh Star (1838)

Craigh, Gerald M.: *Upper Canada* (London, 1963)

Creighton, D. G.: *John A. Macdonald: The Young Politician* (Toronto, 1952)

Dent, C. J.: *The Story of the Upper Canadian Rebellion* (Toronto, 1885)

Guillet, Edwin C.: *The Lives and Times of the Patriots: Early Life in Upper Canada* (Toronto, 1933)

Heustis, Capt., David D.: *A Narrative of the Adventures and Sufferings,* etc. (Boston, 1847)

Hough, T. B.: *A History of St Lawrence and Franklin Counties* (New York, 1856)

Lizars, R. and Macfarlane, K.: *The Days of the Canada Company* (Toronto, 1897)

Mackenzies Gazette

Macleod, A.: *A Brief Review of the Settlement of Upper Canada* (1841)

The Mirror (Toronto, 1839)

Onondaga Centennial: *Gleanings of a Century,* by D. H. Bruce (1896)

Pringle, J. F.: *Lunenburgh or the Old Eastern District, its Settlement and Early Pumpers* (1890)

Richardson, Major J.: *Eight Years in Canada* (Montreal, 1847)

Salina Sentinel

Syracuse Union: *Geschichte der Deutschen in Syracuse und Onondaga County*

Syracuse Gazette

Struthers, Irving E.: *The Trial of Niles von Schoultz* (*Canadian Magazine,* 1917)

Theller, E. A.: *Canada in 1837–1838*

Upper Canada Herald (1838–9)

Way, Ronald N.: *Old Fort Henry, The Citadel of Upper Canada* (Toronto, 1950)

THE FAMILY OF NILS GUSTAF VON SCHOULTZ
Lt. Col. Fredrik Von Schoultz, 1732-1803. *m.* (1766) = Regina Christina Kellander, 1741-1811

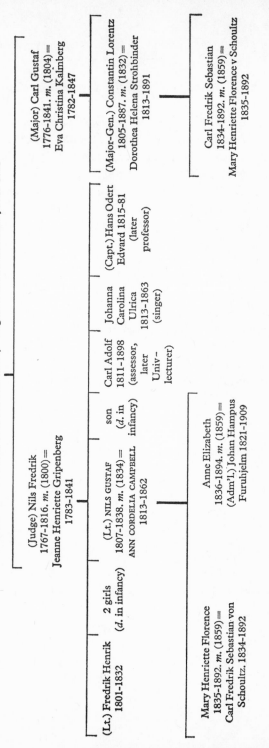

(Judge) Nils Fredrik 1767-1816. *m.* (1800) = Jeanne Henriette Gripenberg 1783-1841

(Major) Carl Gustaf 1776-1841. *m.* (1804) = Eva Christina Kalmberg 1782-1847

(Lt.) Fredrik Henrik 1801-1832

2 girls (*d.* in infancy)

(Lt.) NILS GUSTAF 1807-1838. *m.* (1834) = ANN CORDELIA CAMPBELL 1813-1862

son (*d.* in infancy)

Carl Adolf 1811-1898 (assessor, later Univ-lecturer)

Johanna Carolina Ulrica 1813-1863 (singer)

(Capt.) Hans Odert Edvard 1815-81 (later professor)

(Major-Gen.) Constantin Lorentz 1805-1887. *m.* (1832) = Dorothea Helena Strohbinder 1813-1891

Mary Henriette Florence 1835-1892. *m.* (1859) = Carl Fredrik Sebastian von Schoultz, 1834-1892

Anne Elizabeth 1836-1894. *m.* (1859) = (Adm'l.) Johan Hampus Furuhjelm 1821-1909

Carl Fredrik Sebastian 1834-1892. *m.* (1859) = Mary Henriette Florence v Schoultz 1835-1892

APPENDIX II

THE FAMILY OF ANN CAMPBELL

Simon Frazer of Fairfield, 1754-1825. *m.* (1781) = Mary MacGregor, 1760-1814.

Mary
1785-1843. *m.* (1811)
Alexander Campbell
1770-1821.
(East India Company)

Ann
1787-1837. *m.* (1st) =
(Major) Andrew Frazer
(*d.* 1812)   (2nd) =
Colonel Henry Cox.

Mary
1817-1863. *m.* (1844) =
Col. Simon Frazer Hannay.

Elizabeth
1783-1856. *m.* (1809) =
Thomas Phillips R.A.
(*d.* 1845)

ANN CORDELIA
1813-1862. *m.* (1834) =
(Lt.) NILS GUSTAF VON SCHOULTZ
1807-1838.